MW00330954

Pathways to the Zodiac

Decoding its Origins
and
History

by

E. R. Winstanley

Strategic Book Group

Strategic Book Group
P.O. Box 333
Durham CT 06422
www.StrategicBookGroup.com

ISBN: 978-1-60976-556-9

For my mother, whose insatiable curiosity and meticulous research made this book possible.

Table of Contents

Signposts

"Ascend with the greatest sagacity from Earth to Heaven,
And then again descend to the Earth,
And unite together the power of things superior of the whole world,
And all obscurity will fly away from you."
—*Smaragdine*, the Emerald Tablet of the Phoenicians

Why was the zodiac formed and by whom? Although the obvious answer for its purpose would seem to be its uses for astrology, no explanations have been given concerning its authors or conception. The general belief is that it started with the Greeks, but indications point to star tables that had their origin thousands of years before. The practices of ancient religious rites that go as far back as the early Neolithic age are interwoven with the zodiac. Its methodical definitions establish rites and rituals that are perpetuated by cults and societies throughout the ages; and many still are maintained in contemporary life. Compelling evidence reveals the mystery of the creation of the zodiac, and a scrutiny of ancient societies and cultures links the past to the present tracing directly back to the zodiac and all that it represented.

Signs and symbols reflect cyclic regeneration, and the zodiac was, in its conception, a methodical means of bringing order to the chaotic rule and dominance of the pantheon of gods who powerfully influenced the lives of the ancients. To what extent does the zodiacal religion affect us today? Amazingly more than you may imagine. Although the use of the zodiac currently is confined to astrological purposes, it was not always so, and it is the history of these variations that is so interesting.

The zodiac, created from the sacred calendar, was a precise method of map making, reading the stars, and foretelling the seasons at a time when writing had not been invented. People relied upon pictorial descriptive messages and interpretations of the powerful priest-kings who could decipher the meaning of the correlation between heaven and earth. Inevitably, these priest-kings wielded enormous power, totally dominating the populace. Comprehending the power and area of authority of the many deities in each region would be enormously beneficial to someone wishing to conquer a country and assume control. Sargon 1ˢᵗ of Akkad, who reigned from about 2334–2279 BC, was such a man. Vastly ambitious, he recognized the potential. To ensure his victories, he realized that by establishing the boundaries of the authority of the various gods and acknowledging their influence, the enormous benefits reaped would greatly reward him in his constant search of vital raw materials with which to trade. Consequently, Sargon was the prime instigator for a comprehensive map of the areas designated to the gods, to define the extent of their rule.

Countless remnants of the old religion remain, and modern life reflects the philosophies and ideologies of the ancients best portrayed by the influence of the zodiacal religion in its initial state, eons before its use for astrology. Many religions are variants of the pagan religion predating most of them. Their flares are recognizable in artifacts, forms of worship, and the very words employed in daily usage. Such a commonplace item as the dollar bill of the United States is a prime example, depicting as it does, a ziggurat topped with the All Seeing Eye of Divine Insight, the name given to Asar-Luhi, a son of Ea, one among many of the gods of the zodiacal religion. Intriguingly, the influence of these pagan gods persists, and for the most part, is an accepted component of modern life with rituals continuing to enact the beliefs of teachers of divine knowledge and long dead philosophers.

Footprints tracking back to prehistory repeat certain themes. These share an underlying connection with the Ancient Mysteries, Pythagoras, Egyptian gods, the Knights Templar, and the Freemasons, linking together the common threads of philosophies, the zodiac being the lynch pin. The rites of symbolic death and resurrection had their origins in the zodiacal year reflecting the sacred calendar of the ancients. Plutarch, the ancient Greek philosopher who was a priest of the Delphic Oracle, and Cicero the famous Greek orator, were Pagan initiates, and other philosophers such as Musaeus, Linus, and Plotinus are among pagan theologians. Plotinus inspired mystics of all persuasions: Paganism, Judaism, Christianity, Islam, and the Gnostics. Certainly, the Knights Templar were fully conversant with astrology and numerology, and passed their knowledge to the Freemasons for whom knowledge of astrology was a prerequisite for their Order. Masonic knowledge dates back to the Ancient Mysteries of the early Egyptians and Babylonians, handed down through the centuries. Benjamin Franklin, John Hancock, and thirteen other signers of the Declaration of Independence were Freemasons, including George Washington. Their morals and ethical objectives were "faith, hope, and charity and a belief in God, the ability of each person to improve, and the equality of all people." Musicians such as Haydn and Mozart sought to "drink from the spring of wisdom to find truth." The Roman Catholic Church condemned Freemasonry in 1738, and even now, relations are less than cordial.

Order from chaos has been the ambition and driving force of humankind from the very earliest beginnings. People depended upon the gods whom they believed created the much-desired order. The vast array of deities represented every aspect of nature and the forces of good and evil. They were critically important to the sustenance and well-being of individuals and nations as a whole. The links between ancient cultures signify this commonality between us all, and the Circle of the Zodiac demonstrates the first attempts to establish a semblance of order to the pattern of daily life. Ancient gods called Sutekh, Sadok, and Zedec who was god of the Night Sky, seem to imply the word *zodiac*. Melchizedek, the lord of the zodiac, was the Amorite name for their priest-kings of the zodiacal religion, and this title, and the ones who held it, is of paramount importance in this study.

Ma'at, the goddess of Truth, Justice, and Order, has been an influence for many cultures over the years, and it is these precepts that embodied the whole way of life for the earliest civilizations. The Sumerians worshipped Anu who, as the Supreme Lord of Heaven, was the source of all law and order. The Qumran Community, the New Church of Jerusalem, the Knights Templar, the Druids and the Freemasons all respected and valued the early teachings of our ancestors, whose ethics and standards of behavior form the basis for our culture today, upholding the qualities of goodness, mercy, and righteousness. Gods and mortals were venerated for their wisdom and teachings. King Solomon, Pythagoras, and Jesus Christ in particular are respected for their remarkable insight and instruction, leaving their powerful mark upon the world. In the search for knowledge and truth, the seeking of the light has always been the primary motivation of humankind. Alexandria was an important center of learning containing the largest library of the time. The mysteries celebrated here were Pagan, and Paganism and Judaism together were part of the traditional religious ceremonies. The Zadokites of Qumran, the Essenes, were the possessors of the secret knowledge. They wore white robes and took vows of poverty. Zadok, the high priest of Jerusalem, anointed Solomon as king. Zadok in Hebrew translates as The Just. The Sons of Zadok, as found in the Dead Sea Scrolls, were referred to as the Sons of Truth and Sons of the Dawn.

The Knights Templar are a key link between the Ancient Mysteries, King Solomon, and the Freemasons. Their esoteric knowledge spread to distant lands, although the Mysteries and Wisdom were known to but a few of their Order. The living quarters of the first Knights were on what had been the site of Solomon's temple. They were convinced that treasure was buried beneath and spent years searching for it. When the Knights renounced the secular world, they virtually abandoned their wives and families. Similar to the Essenes they took vows of poverty and chastity, and wore white surcoats emblazoned with a distinctive red cross to signify their purity and membership of the Order. Nevertheless, despite their vows, the Templars accumulated great riches, tantalizing scores of treasure hunters who believe they are hidden away awaiting discovery.

Erected according to very precise instructions, the temple of

Solomon was an earthly dwelling place for Yahweh. It was an amazing feat of construction and Solomon's outstanding achievement. Built by architects and laborers who shared the vision of a sacred purpose that was to unify the tribes, they sought to achieve a balance between the highest and lowest of Solomon's empire. Two famous pillars stood before it: Jachin/Tsedeq and Boaz/Mishpat placed over nine hidden vaults. The land of Israel was represented by the two pillars, which, when combined with the holy arch Shalom, became the Gate of Righteousness. Buried deep beneath the temple, inscribed on sacred scrolls, was the Wisdom of the Ages, part of the treasure sought by the Templars.

King Solomon worshipped Jehovah, and the goddess Astoreth (Ishtar), maintaining the religion of the zodiac, keeping a balance for his subjects, and not taking any chances. Purportedly, he was a Grand Master of Freemasonry, and modern Freemasonry links its order to the Ancient Mysteries. The origin of the Freemasons seems to be in North Africa, because when Prince Edward, son of Henry the Third of England established this society, they called themselves The Order of the Architects of Africa. However, the origins and legends are a constant source of speculation and debate. The people who lived then were enlightened, spiritually conscious, and sensitive, as Freemasons throughout the years have aspired to be. Countless ways demonstrate these links, and the use of pillars in sacred places is a substantial connection, playing an important role in our history.

Pillars feature prominently for Freemasons for whom symbolism is an integral part of the Order. The Pillars of Freemasonry represent the pillars of Solomon's temple, and are prominent and vital signs, reminding their members of the qualities of the kingly and priestly messiahs. The pillars, one of marble and one of brick, are at the entrance to the circle: Jachin for masculine, positive, establishment, and stability; and Boaz, feminine, negative, and for all things righteous. The Archives of Masonry are inscribed on the brick column, and the marble pillar bears an inscription claiming a treasure is buried beneath it. To create order within themselves, the Freemasons use symbolic principles of the square, level, and plumb rule. To aspire to the Ultimate Truth and Light,

5

they endure the symbolic death of self-imperfections to rise up to a renewal of life, and as such are builders. God is the Master Builder. The ancient peoples venerated God as the center of all light and energy who ruled by a fixed law and was perfect, a light shining in the darkness. Light to the Ancients meant not only "other than darkness," but also true knowledge. The Freemasons allude to a central point within a circle, and Shamash, the Babylonian sun god, is that center of the zodiacal circle.

Mystics have revered rock formations since the beginning of time. These awesome megalithic dolmens and circles of stones found everywhere raise questions as to their significance and the role they played in the lives of our forbears. Erected on sites where the builders believed the Earth Spirit moves, they appear in diverse locations. The circles of stones were the earliest forms of worship, and had many uses as temples, gathering places of worship, counsel, and fortification. There are countless markers telling a story of incredible people who lived, and worshipped the gods of their time, recording their rituals and methods of veneration in everlasting memorials of stone. Histories of the stones demonstrate unbelievably sophisticated technology and expertise that we are still unable to comprehend fully or even imitate. Stone circles were strategically placed to harmonize the magnetic force of the earth; the builders believed these circles would attract the various deities, who would then inhabit the carefully selected places. Built on high ground to be seen from a great distance, the circles served as a spiritual meeting place for the wandering tribes.

The world's first temple, an exciting discovery recently unearthed in Turkey, dates from 12,000 years ago. It comprises a series of huge megaliths forming circles. Ten to fifty ton t-shaped stone pillars stand at the site. They probably represented the Tau cross that has played a key role in the worship of the gods from the earliest times. Animals of all descriptions depicted on the pillars, make a connection to the Greek words *zodiakos kyklos*, which is animal circle, and *UL.HE*, Sumerian for Shiny Herd.

Marveling at these great edifices around the world, and Stonehenge in particular, which also has t-shaped stones, the impact of the legacy of the stones is stunning. Their silent grandeur holds the key to our past. Reflecting the beliefs and rituals of the people who built them, they are veritable signposts pointing us to the road of exploration. The extensive alignments of stones at Carnac in France are from the early Neolithic era dating from around 4500 BC. Some, placed in rows, extend for about a mile, while others, laid out in circles, are in alignment with the sun and the moon, probably used for both astronomical and astrological purposes. Found in so many locations, these strange circles of stones indicate a common link between the ancients. Their comprehension of the movement of the stars and their reverence for the cosmos was recorded for all time.

The first references to gods found in cave paintings in France and Spain, reveal that the Cro-Magnons worshipped the Great Mother Astarte/Ishtar, and the Great Father Ba'al/Bel, two of the greatest among the pantheon of the Babylonian gods. Baalbeck was a temple to the great god Bel. Vast blocks of stone were transported from miles away for its construction, and the similar search for the appropriate stones for other temples reinforces our admiration of the single-minded purpose and indomitable spirit of our ancestors.

It begs the questions of who were the architects, from whence came their knowledge, and what was the driving force that inspired such incredible feats? The instigators who envisaged such remarkable enterprises managed to coerce thousands of workers to promote their ideologies. The attraction of these monuments connects and binds us together in our search for the answers to these mysteries.

The circles of stones usually are remnants of megalithic temples where a priest invokes the spirit of the god. The Vatican was built on the site of such a temple. Various paintings depict the Virgin Mary and the virgin Saint Genevieve sitting inside circles of stones. These were the earliest forms of religious sites. Many hilltop chapels correspond with the ancient gods of the pagan rites. The serpent, as a representative of the zodiac, is highly symbolic, and some stone circles portray it encircling them to signify the earth. Numerous references in the Bible point to the importance of the circle in the ancient religion. Joshua chapters four and five tell about the Israelites setting up camp at Gilgal (great circle) with twelve boundary stones they had brought with them out of Jordan. Was their purpose to define the territories of each of the twelve tribes of Israel? Boundary stones were essential to establish the territory of the tribes who wandered the ancient lands. The chart that Sargon created is still in use by the Chinese to this day. His chart shows several *biru* (borough or burgh) in relation to a mountain in the approximate position of Mount Ararat, which at that time was regarded as the summit of the earth.

Whole cities constructed in exact symmetrical designs acted as a powerful invocation for worshippers of their ancient religion. Some cities, laid out in the precise way of a circle in which the axis represented the sun and the center of the universe, reflected ancient cosmology. The foundations of many cities depict the zodiacal design, and yet another has recently become known which displays these particular markings or boundaries within the city with definite segments radiating from the circle at the center. From the Celtic cross foundations of a fishing village in Mexico to the circular walls and wedge-like partitions of Al Rawda in Syria and the plan of Firuzabad in Iran, the fundamental structure of zodiacal proportions can be recognized, and the philosophies of their founders construed.

From the dawn of history, mathematical formulae, regarded as a sacred art, were essential to the construction of cities, monuments, and temples. The completion of these sites, with such exact measurements and size, staggers the imagination. In particular, the Babylonians were extremely painstaking about the placement of their buildings. In many cultures, astrologers and astronomers determine the most fortuitous place for the masons to lay the corner stone for the foundations. The precise placement of buildings and places of worship on earth in relation to the heavens was essential not only for the community to flourish, but to accord the appropriate veneration of the gods for whom they were devised.

The Bedouins of the Persian Gulf, the wandering tribes of the Middle East, the Sumerians, the Babylonians, and ancient Australians all shared the mystical belief in spirits who inhabited all forms of the natural world—rocks and stones, trees and animals—the cult of the earth spirit in its many guises.

Mystery enshrouds many manmade stone markers and edifices. They defy explanation until we connect them with the zodiacal religion. The Sphinx is undoubtedly the foremost among them, because everything points to it being a zodiacal monument. It represents the four cardinal points of the compass and the cross within the circle of the zodiac. This enigmatic edifice could well be the symbol for Nebo, the Winged Man, with the human head representing Aquarius/Water; the body of a bull represents Bel/Taurus, the Earth; the paws of a lion for Leo/Fire, the Winged Lion, Shamash the Sun; and the wings of an eagle for Scorpio/ Air ruled by Ninib. This symbolizes the constellations of Leo and its opposite house, Aquarius. The implication of these symbols cannot be stressed enough—the four figures of the book of Revelation in the Bible were the lion, the ox, the man, and the eagle. The Sphinx faces the eastern horizon where the sun rises in the spring and autumn equinoxes, and is associated with Horus the sun god. It is believed by many to have been built in the age of Leo, and geologists are convinced that the Sphinx must have been built before the last period of flooding in the Sahara at least 12,000 years ago. Was the Sphinx a marker or indicator of significant importance to divine beings of past ages? Possibly it is a sign for others to use in conjunction with the map of the zodiac because of its precise location to the pyramids on earth and their relation to the stars above. Alternatively, did it serve as a star gate mechanism of some kind? Undoubtedly, the Sphinx is a mysterious legacy, perhaps demonstrating something extraordinary that happened thousands of years ago, and perhaps will occur again at some pre- ordained time. Such conjectures, which tease the imagination, are not beyond the realm of possibility.

If the pyramids of Egypt were built earlier than the current wisdom implies, then the fact of their meticulous placing and undeniably superior design require would the use of highly technical mathematical formulae. They also were aligned with the four cardinal points: north, south, east and west, but for what purpose? Stone builders were motivated by their concern for the well-being of the dead in the after-life, believing that their precise construction was a method for the soul to be directed heavenwards, leaving the corpse buried within. The earliest decans and charts of the original zodiac may have served as guideposts for a much earlier civilization, long before Sargon compiled the knowledge into the map as we know it today. Did they, in conjunction with the Sphinx, direct earthly beings to their heavenly ancestors?

Ancient stones erected over sacred health-giving springs of water were reputed to house a spirit, and temples were built for that same intention. The austere megaliths of Stonehenge are some of the most well-known examples of ancient stone circles. Of awesome size and precision these structures corresponding with the planets, were erected relative to the earth spirit that flowed beneath. Some believe that Thoth, the Egyptian god of mathematics, astronomy, magic, botany, and medicine, was the designer of Stonehenge, which served as a zodiacal guide for the measurement of time. Thoth, accredited with not only the invention of figures, the letters of the alphabet, and the seven vowels, may have known the secrets of the heavens, which were inscribed in sacred books. Perhaps he truly is the one to whom the credit belongs. Stonehenge was a pagan temple, a center of trade and learning for the Heraclids, and above all, a place for healing because it was built in an area that is reputed to have healing properties ascribed to the earth spirit moving beneath. There appears to be a unified system of knowledge of this spirit that passes through the countryside in particular seasons determined by the positions of the heavenly bodies. The structure of Stonehenge would therefore have been of critical importance to the well being of the populace, whose lives were directed by the sacred calendar. It is a formidable signpost for the spiritual phenomena at this site. The circular design has within its boundaries four post holes. The four points within the circle represent the four quarters of the compass, the cross, and the four cherubim, all reflecting the influence of the four ruling astral gods. The pillars and crossbeam, the Tau cross, and many other symbolic structures that abound at Stonehenge reinforce the zodiacal imprint. The trilithons erected within the Sarsen Circle form a horseshoe with the open ends facing the northeast. The altar stone is placed in front of the central and largest of the trilithons. Were these representations of the pillars of the Bible through which worshippers must pass to pay homage to the deity?

The recent discovery of the remains of village life dating from around 2600 BC displays a temporary wooden circle, which may have symbolized life, whereas the stones of Stonehenge symbolize death. This wooden circle, aligning as it does with the sunrise at the winter solstice, confirms what many have conjectured for years that the whole complex has astronomical and astrological connotations. The themes of life, death, and renewal were the driving forces of the builders of these edifices, concluding that Stonehenge was one of the most inspiring remains, if not the largest. Such compelling evidence emphasizes a religion in which the zodiac plays an integral role. A double ring of stones denotes the exclusive burial place of the Amorite priest-kings, and these signs are found not only here, but also in other similar structures. The modern day Druids use the site for their rituals, revering Stonehenge as their temple of worship, drawn to the mythical aura permeating it.

The familiar white horses carved into the hills in Britain are a reminder of the influence of the Heraclidae to whom white horses were sacred. Did the circular setting of a hundred stake holes found at Stonehenge serve as tethering posts for their horses? These tribes came to Britain to trade by way of rivers and would have needed the headwaters of these streams to provide water for their cherished animals.

The Heraclidae were trading all over Europe from as early as 2460 BC, although the Amurru had had trading camps there long before, bringing their form of worship with them. These were the Amurru (Amorites) and the Hurri (Horites) who together ruled Egypt as the Heraclid Dynasty, which lasted from 2460 BC to 2040 BC. The Giant at Cerne Abbas represents the father figure, and with his raised phallus was the symbol of the Heraclidae. An interesting tradition has it that if young brides sat there they would bear many children. Who knows, perhaps this practice is still continued. This giant carved into the hills is brandishing a club that seems to be pointing the way, but to where and why? Giants were known to the ancients and are still around. The Israelites in Canaan saw giants (Numbers 13:22–33) and the Amorites were looked upon as the giants of the Bible. In Britain many earthworks can be found depicting the signs of the zodiac. The most famous is at Glastonbury in the West Country not far from Stonehenge. This Land Zodiac is remarkable because, like many other earthworks worldwide,

11

it can be best appreciated from the air. The signs, marked out by tracks and streams correspond to their heavenly counterparts, and must surely have been the work of giants. Were they aided by the gods? These incredible land markings provide further proof of the zodiacal influence, and contribute to the mysticism pervading much of not only the English countryside, but countless locations on this planet.

Worldwide, tremendous carefully placed stones represent reverence for a deity. The best-known and most sacred stone for the Muslims is the black-draped Ka'ba stone building within the mosque at Mecca. Originally, it was part of the cult of the worship of Cybele, the great mother goddess of the Phrygians, whose followers believed that they would be reborn to a new life after death. The Ka'ba symbolized the meeting of heaven and earth. Long before the advent of the prophet Mohammed, the shrine contained images of gods and goddesses, and for early worshipers the stone promised good fortune and prosperity. The Dome of the Rock, built in AD 691 by the Muslims to honor Mohammad, is the earliest surviving example of Islamic architecture. It is on the site of the Temple of the Jews. The Dome, a source of veneration for the Abrahamic trinity of Christians, Jews, and Muslims alike, is a most exquisite example of Islamic art. The design of the dome conveys the symbolism of the circle and the geometry of sacred mathematical formulae. Another famous dome is that of St. Paul's Cathedral in London whose designer, Christopher Wren, was a Grand Master Mason of the Order of Freemasons whose signs and symbols reflect the teachings of the Gnostics and the Knights Templar.

The symbolic circle, representing the cosmos and eternity, is acknowledged worldwide. Ancient Native Americans had a cosmically ordered society, and the Hopi tribe especially reveres the circle and the spiritual powers within it. Their worship of the Great Spirit mirrors the worship of the Babylonians who believed *zi* (spirit) peopled the world.

Pillars are predominant markers because they have emphasized sanctity since the very beginning of recorded history, being suggestive of power and mysticism. They feature prominently in many sacred buildings and credit goes to the Sumerians for creating them as a way of reaching to the heavens. The history of pillars is fundamental to this search. Found throughout the world, they appear with regularity in most structures built for the express purpose of worship. The very name of the Sumerian city, Babylon, is indicative of Sumerian religion—*bab* means gate, and *ilu* of the gods. The Old Testament often refers to pillars. Jacob's anointed pillar was at Bethel (House of God) and interestingly, the name Jacob is the Sumerian word for pillar. Exodus 13:21 stresses their importance: "And the Lord went before them by day in a pillar of a cloud, to lead them the way; and by night a pillar of fire, to give them light; to go by day and night." The Pillars of Hermes, the protector of travelers, mark the ways leading them to the center of the city. The Egyptians knew the people of the area between the Nile Delta and Moab, the Hebrews, as Hiru-shaitu, the Hurri. This snippet is mentioned because the important link to the zodiacal religion lies in the fact that the doors to their towers, the Pillars of Heru, are precisely similar to those of Stonehenge. Traditionally, the Pillars of Hercules were the pillars set up by the first Phoenicians. Hathor, the Egyptian Mother Goddess, was revered as the Lady of the Pillar. A pillar with a fish on top of her head represents Hamhit as the queen of all the gods. The Pillars of Upper and Lower Egypt, united by a heavenly crossbeam, symbolize the unification of the two kingdoms.

The Rosslyn Chapel, a mystical building in Scotland, teems with symbolism. *Ros* means ancient knowledge and *lyn* means generation. Founded about AD 1446, this extraordinary chapel of eccentric design bears the marks of many cults; the Knights Templar and the Freemasons are but two examples. Some claim that Rosslyn is a replica of the ruins of Herod's Temple built to resemble Solomon's Temple, while others vehemently oppose this idea. Still more are convinced that the chapel contains the famous scrolls of Solomon, and so the debates continue. Rosslyn has twelve pillars plus the two main pillars of Boaz and Jachin. All the pillars are perpetual reminders of the links between the houses of the gods of the zodiac, the twelve apostles, and the twelve tribes of Israel. Supposedly, there are many hidden messages of the Templars incorporated into this intriguing building. Their seal bears their symbol of two riders on a single horse. Other philosophies from the Ancient Mysteries, Gnostic teachings, Kabbalah wisdom, and the zodiacal religion are portrayed within Rosslyn's walls. Aloe, cactus plants, and maize cobs carved into various lintels and arches of the chapel are surprising because the plants were unknown in Europe in 1446. They may have been a tribute to the Maize Goddess of the western hemisphere. The discovery of a grave in North America bearing all the telltale markings of a Templar is proof of a visit by the Knights. The evening star, Venus, called the Star of the West, indicated a special place known to them as Merica.

There are countless connections between the Knights Templar and the Freemasons. The Templars based their teachings on the original Jerusalem Church and the Ancient Mysteries preceding it. The combination of the rituals of the Freemasons who followed is continually impressed in myriads of ways. The Templars were renowned for their circular churches and their eight-pointed cross, a symbol for the goddess Ishtar/Venus. Many chapels reflect the influence of the zodiac because they depict the twelve apostles alongside the twelve signs of the zodiac with Christ at the center of the circle, although in the zodiacal form it is Shamash the Sun who is the center as the Giver of Light.

Many words in contemporary usage link to the zodiac when translated: one is the Hebrew word *tzaddiq* that translates as a just or righteous man who takes joy in justice. He is a religious leader viewed as a mediator between man and God. From this word *tzaddiq,* others are closely associated: *tsedeq*; *Sydyk*, the eighth god; zodiac; *zedec* whom the Canaanites associated with the sun; and importantly, James the Just, the brother of Jesus, Teacher of Righteousness. James wore a bishop's mitre copied from a crown of Amon-Ra the creator god of Thebes, the city that provided ancient Judaism with the central tenets of its theology. Ra was the Holy One, the Falcon of the Horizon. The name of the high priest Josedek means divine righteousness, and is linked to the Eighth God, who is Jupiter. The connections are there to be deciphered more conclusively.

The ancient market for papyrus was Byblos/Gebal, the Amorite religious center, and the word bible derives from this. Gibil is the ancient fire god of Ur, and Gebal is identified with him. Galil means circle. Galilee, Gilgal, and Galileo all stem from the word for circle. It is quite an amazing coincidence that Galileo is the name of the very man who promoted the concept of the earth circling the sun. Galileo translates as circle and sun.

Supposedly, the mountains were the dwelling places of the deity, and should none be nearby, imitations were created to house them. Called ziggurats (ziggurat: *zi* is spirit, *kir* is earth) they consisted of seven blocks rising to the heavens. Earthly sanctuaries for the gods take many forms, from the earliest stone circles to the imposing cathedrals of our day.

Most cathedrals are built in a cruciform ground plan with the axis east to west and the internal emphasis on the eastern end where the altar is placed. The construction of the early European cathedrals in particular demonstrates the specific architecture that incorporates two pillars at the west end, drawing worshippers into the holy place down the nave towards the east. Westminster Abbey, York Minster in England, and Notre Dame in Paris are prime examples of this particular design. The nave (Latin for ship) is where worshippers congregate. The ship features prominently in legends—as in the Arc of Heaven, whose pilot Ursa Nebo traversed the heavens, and Noah's Ark of the Great Flood. An intriguing premise is that some of these impressive cathedrals were specifically aligned with Orion as markers to be coordinated with the precise alignment of the Sphinx.

Intricately interwoven, these legends are difficult to unravel. Scores of names converge in the tapestry, but the core remains with the zodiac as the basis for reconstruction. So many traditions sharing the same roots are veritable signposts for us to decipher the wisdom of the ancients. From the earliest times, they sought to record the movement of the stars and the cycle of the natural world. The zodiac was perhaps the greatest record of all. To be able to recognize the importance of it as it continues to affect our daily life, we must go back to its earliest beginnings with the Amorites and Melchizedek, their Lord High Priest of the Zodiac.

Melchizedek and Other Mysteries

Imagine a thriving metropolis with a splendid library, a magnificent temple to the goddess Ishtar, and a sumptuous palace with walls richly adorned. In the kitchens, pastries were baked in fancy molds, and ice was imported for not only maintaining fresh vegetables and fruits at their peak, but also to ensure the flavor of food and wine as it was brought to the table. The keeping of a good table was a matter of prestige. Game, fish, honey, truffles, and locusts were among the many delicacies, and the wine was stored in refrigerated cellars.

Administrators of this cultural center were muscular people having reddish hair, wide cheekbones, and of considerable stature, wearing rich jewelry and pearls. Who were these highly intellectual people? The Amurru, the Amorites of the Bible. Through archeology, whole nations have been recognized that for many were merely names mentioned in the Bible. The history of the Amorites only becomes clear when certain facts from texts and letters appear in the various countries where they had been. They emerge as a very important part of early history—one might call them the father race of most Europeans, and their records developed slowly as an elusive feature of historical beginnings.

The Amurru were the original race of people whose history is traced back to Cro-Magnon, the Aurignacians, who inhabited the Atlas Mountains, the area known as the Fertile Crescent: Mesopotamia, Egypt, Iran, and the Persian Gulf. They were among the world's first mariners,

16

had widespread connections with each other, and were well established in trade as far apart as Britain, Bahrain, Denmark, Lebanon, and Bokhara. They called themselves "an ancient litter" even then. Could they have been the Atlanteans of the legends of the Dinaric race of whom the Albanians are the living remnants? In Tidanim (The Lebanon) the Amurru were known as Tidanu (Murik Tidmin) or Danu, first men. These were the giants of the Bible, which mentions them as "a people apart from others," as does Xenophon, the ancient Greek philosopher and historian. Others held them in considerable awe, and it is no wonder they merited the title The Sons of Heaven. Golden regalia from Byblos found in Egyptian tombs would most likely have belonged to the Amorites when they ruled Egypt, conveying the message of their supremacy. They compiled the star tables sought by Sargon who did battle with them in order to acquire them. The *Texts of Ugarit* implies that this was the religion of these peoples.

Melchizedek was the name given by the Amorites for their high priest of their ancient pagan religion, which was a hereditary title held by them. The Amorite priest-kings were called Adonai Zedec (Lord of Justice,) and Melchi-Zedek. Melchizedek was the priest-king of Jerusalem. He is mentioned in the Dead Sea Scrolls: "For I have a name: I am Melchizedek, the Priest of God Most High; I know that it is I who am truly the image of the true High Priest of God Most High." *Melchi* means lord, and *zedek* has many interpretations: god of the Night Sky, Jupiter; Sydyk, the Eighth God; justice; righteousness; and zodiac. Quoting from the *International Standard Bible Encyclopedia,* "The Amarna and Ras Shamrah parallels suggest, however, that the original meaning was 'my king is righteous,' 'my (the) king is Zedek (a deity) is righteous.'" Zedek is the sun god, and god of the night sky is Jupiter. Zaddik priests were teachers of Kabbalah. Thus, Melchizedek was Lord of the Zodiac, who worshipped El Elyon, God Most High.

Abram, later known as Abraham, was a highly educated man in the Babylonian sciences of astronomy and mathematics, and Chaldean astrology. So venerated by followers of Christianity, Judaism, and Islam alike, he creates the Abrahamic trinity of these three religions. At first he lived in Ur, the Amorite center of pagan culture that exerted tremendous influence, where there was a ziggurat to the moon goddess Nanna. When the Amurru left Ur, Abraham went with them to Haran and thence to Jerusalem where he acknowledged Melchizedek as Yahweh giving him "a tenth of the spoils" (Hebrews 7). Abraham's priesthood links with Melchizedek. Abraham was partially responsible for the building of the sanctuary of God in Mecca. He was the first prophet of the true God and regarded as the first Muslim because he practiced obedience, which is the primary tenet of Islam. Islam, an ancient faith, is considerably older than Christianity or Judaism. Abraham is mentioned in the Koran more times than any other biblical figure. His association with Melchizedek is compelling evidence of the enormous influence wielded by this formidable priest-king of the Amorites.

The history of the personage of Melchizedek is tantalizingly sketchy. The archangel Michael supposedly rescued him from the deluge by taking him to Eden. He identifies with Shem, one of Noah's sons, who received the land of Israel from Noah to rule. If we compare him to those who followed bearing this title, the conclusion may be drawn that it was not just one person, but also many people who perpetuated and embodied this dedicated position of priest of priests of the sacred priesthood. Melchizedek is the eternal priesthood. He was the King of Peace, and Paul referred to him as the King of Righteousness. Jesus was a priest of this Order (Hebrews 6, also in Genesis 14; Psalm 110, and the Epistle to the Hebrews). Melchizedek is also Michael - light and truth. Priests make their final vows to the church using the Order of Melchizedek, which is valid for life. For some, the Order of Melchizedek encompasses all religions of both East and West.

The gospels of Matthew and Luke refer to Jesus as being of the line of David, who, as a priestly king, traced his lineage through David to Melchizedek. When David captured Jerusalem, the royal priesthood of Melchizedek was conferred upon him, acknowledging his unique position with God as a priest-king. This new priesthood was far superior to the Levitical priesthood, indeed some Jews saw Melchizedek as the new Messiah. According to the Epistle to the Hebrews, he was "Without father, without mother, without descent, having neither beginning of days nor end of life; but was made like unto the Son of God, abideth a

18

priest continually." St. Paul says, "Even Jesus made an high priest forever after the order of Melchizedek." Jesus conferred the apostles with this priesthood, and they in turn conferred it upon others. According to Scripture, Melchizedek is the only priest who dispensed with the slaughter of animals on the altar as the sacrificial offering, introducing the idea of bread and blood as the replacement. From the earliest times, the eating of corn constituted a sacrament and may have been beneficial to partakers in the belief they were consuming the divinity that flowed through the bread. Melchizedek, depicted in the magnificent cathedrals of both Chartres and Rheims, in France, is holding a cup, seemingly conveying a message that predates the holy cup of Jesus, because the cup as a symbol for Aquarius, represented eternal life long before Christ walked the earth.

Throughout history, Melchizedek has been a forceful influence, and many have been, and still are, closely associated with him. Starting with Bel, the Babylonian deity who also was Lord of the Zodiac and known as Melchizedek, then with the Amorites, Abraham, and those of the lineage of King David. The association continues with the Knights Templar and the Freemasons and now with the present day Mormon Church, and the Ancient Mystic Order of Melchizedek, founded in 1967. Such is the power of this high priest of the Amorites, who is perpetuated through his ancient symbols: the chalice with the loaf of bread.

Chaos is the law of nature, and order and harmony are the dream of humankind. The Ancient Mysteries, rituals, and worship of numerous gods and goddesses demonstrate the reliance of our ancestors upon the deities to regulate their lives. The early civilizations believed that gods fought against the beings that were responsible for the chaos, so when the gods triumphed they were venerated for bestowing the benefits of order. The gods conceived divine laws, the Me's, which governed humankind, and the universe. These laws were complex, relating to the peoples' various political, social, and religious institutions, and covering all aspects of artistic and emotional behavior. Sumerian mythology refers to these laws and the influence of the gods who were obeyed in humility by the mortals who worshipped them. The Mesopotamian story of creation refers to Ti'amat the dragon and Bel, the Lord of the Earth who fought him to overcome chaos to create order. His mission was to restore the world to the order in which it was perfected by the earliest gods; however, the constant warring between these gods frequently wrought chaos causing further turbulence.

To better understand the gods and the influence they exerted, we must analyze the roles they played and their position in the zodiac. The great triad of Babylonian gods was Anu, Ea, and Bel. At the time of the creation of the zodiac, around 2732 BC, there were four astral gods who represented the four known planets and the four cherubim: Bel, Nergal, Ninib, and Nebo. Bel was Jupiter and the Winged Bull of the Compass; Nergal, Lord of Death, was Mars and represented the Sun as the Winged Lion of the Zodiac; Ninib, Lord of Justice and Air represented Saturn; and Nebo, God of Water, Intellect and Medicine was the Winged Man.

Anu, as the supreme Lord of Heaven, was the source of all law and order. As such, he presided over the assembly of the gods, and was referred to as the King of the Annunaki, the gods who lived on earth and in the Underworld. Anu ruled Aquarius, the House of Creation, the House of Heaven (Heofan—House of Anu) the home of the gods to which they retreated from the noise of humankind. The land of Shu held up the heaven and divided heaven and earth. El, called Ilu, the father of the gods, dwelt here. The *Texts of Ugarit* tells of his home being at the sources of the two rivers, in the midst of the great streams—the Two Great Deeps. The mountain Ararat, considered the summit of the earth, was where heaven and earth met. Holy Ararat stood as a symbol with its perpetual head of white snow from which a plume of white smoke still issues reminding people of the awesome power that lies within this mountain of the gods. The great sun god Shamash rose from his eastern gate of heaven (the Caspian Sea) bringing the dawn on his daily traverse across the earth. Heaven was thought to be the beautiful lake called Van. Lying more than 5,400 feet above sea level, it is a deep blue. It is eighty miles long and fifty miles at its greatest width; flowing between Aklat and Van. Surrounded by high mountains, which in places reach the level of perpetual snow, Lake Van is mostly placid, although at times it has great waves. Upon its banks are orchards, meadows, and gardens unequalled for beauty anywhere.

20

Eventually, Anu left his House on earth to retreat heavenwards, becoming known as The Faraway or Dios, and Nebo replaced him, as the Winged Man, Aquarius.

Ea, the second god in this triad, was the eldest son of Anu begotten in his own image. He was the god of supreme wisdom, spells, and charms, and of arts and crafts. Ea organized the earth, and it is he who is given credit for creating the Circle of the Zodiac because he seems to have been the one responsible for the appointment and deposition of celestial rulers. He set up boundaries and placed Utu/Shamash the Sun God in charge of them, placing Shamash in the middle of the circle with the gods surrounding him. Ea was a leader of the Annunaki, as was Shamash. The Pagans' Solar Cult worshiped Shamash as the source of light and life. High moral and ethical conduct was established, which promoted the concept of a personal deity to whom one could call for help and relief from the perils of the world. Ea, the original Sumerian god of water who is Aquarius, holds a vase from which two streams of water flow, representing the Tigris and the Euphrates, which rise in the Caucasus and join at the Gulf. Ea is Hua the Serpent of the Zodiac, who encircles it with his tail in his mouth as the symbol of eternal life. This powerful god held the rank of forty in the hierarchical system, and when Nebo as the ruler of Aquarius displaced him, the House of Pisces became Ea's dwelling place.

Bel, a supreme and mighty deity, was the third in the great triad of gods. Bel was Melchizedek, the Lord of the Zodiac, who charted the heavens and earth, and the formation of the zodiac. He is also Jupiter, Zeus, Earth, Zedec, Sadok and Sutekh. His power was so immense that he boasted four arks or tabernacles, and four Houses or regions of influence. There is a story of Bel's visit to El in the Caucasus, the god's house on earth, where he is delivered to Yamm (Pisces) as a slave. Imprisoned for the odd days over the 360 degrees of a circle, he is resurrected again when the sun resumes his annual journey around the zodiac. Bel will be reborn in The House of the Sea, to become the Young Bull—the earth in spring, where he is now referred to as the Bull of Heaven and Earth. The Bull is the force of reproduction that fertilizes the land from which all humankind is created and to which all will return. Bel is the ruler of the House of Taurus.

The *Enuma Elish* is the Babylonian epic of creation, the whole of which the priests recited at the festival of Nisan when the sun passed from the House of Pisces, where Bel has ruled. The chanting of this hymn supposedly aided Bel in his yearly combat with Ti'amat and the chaos the spring floods brought. On the fifth or ninth day of Nisan, the destinies of the land were determined for the ensuing year.

In order that all the gods might have their image visible in the sky, Bel mapped out the vault of heaven with groups of stars which he allotted to them. These groups were the constellations, and all who lived on earth were represented in the Arc of Heaven as a mirror and a record. The precession of the days was under the authority of Niburu, the Ferryman, and so none should wander from the track and be lost, Bel lighted the moon that she might rule the night. She was the star of the night who indicated the days from month to month without ceasing. Bel, as Lord of the Zodiac, is possibly the most important figure in its history, and as its lord, gave constellations to Nergal, Ninib, Nebo, and Ishtar, reserving Jupiter for himself.

Nergal, the Winged Lion or Sun of Death, is the ruler of Leo. Twin lions represent Leo; one for the sun and the other symbolizes Nergal, the Lofty Dragon Beloved of Ekur. Nergal had many symbols depending upon his role; for example, when the Romans called him Mars, the cock was his symbol and his helmet sported cock feathers. As Nera, his symbol became the Golden Fleece worn by the Philistines, Caryians and Illyrians. Gold adhered to fleece washed in rivers running with gold. The Greeks identified Aries with a golden fleece suspended in the Grove of Ares that Jason managed to capture, even though it was guarded by the dragon Cetus.

The great god Ninib, Lord of Justice and Air, was the ruler of Saturn, the last planet to enter the zodiac, and although his own house is Scorpio, he rules Capricorn with his wife Rhea, the goddess of Capricorn, and they have a son, Nebo. (This is confusing because some legends maintain that Bel was Rhea's husband and Nebo's father, further demonstrating the intertwining of these deities, and their names.) Eventually Anu and Ninib ruled together as Uranus and Saturn. The realm of Ninib covered

Scorpio and Sagittarius in addition to Capricorn, which is the eastern side of the zodiac. Ninib, ruling both Libra and Scorpio, is the eagle-headed serpent that represents the good and evil of this world. His totem is Ningursu, an eagle holding two lions back to back in his talons.

The Winged Man, Nebo, has all the attributes of Ea, the god of water, and as the god of supreme intelligence, water and medicine, he is closely associated with both Hermes the winged messenger, and Thoth the impressive Egyptian god. Although Nebo's house is Virgo, he is born in Capricorn whose great star was Mah and whose mother goddess was Rhea. One cannot overlook the extraordinary coincidence of Mah-Rhea, especially when one considers Nebo's destiny and his role as the representative of Man in the zodiac.

The Chaldean empire was powerful in 747 BC. The Chaldeans were the Amurru and the Kassites who had formed a nation in the islands of the Persian Gulf. They reorganized the zodiac and forced the Assyrians, whose empire was falling, to elevate Nebo from his House of Virgo and place him in the House of Aquarius. This was done for him to represent man in all three Houses of Aquarius, Pisces, and Capricorn. As the ruler of Aquarius he became Ursa Nebo, the Ferryman who guides souls across from the House of Heaven to Pisces, the last House of the sun's journey around the zodiac. Pisces is the House of Death and Resurrection where Nebo is ordained to die. Just as Bel died and was reborn in Pisces, so the sacred king must be slain and born again. The king was purified, as all must be who "pass over the bridge*"* When the sun had completed the 360 degrees of the zodiacal cycle, the temples were cleansed on the fifth day. The king rested for the odd days and then he passed over to the House of Aries to begin his journey once again.

Chronus rules Capricorn, bestowing the god Taaut/Thoth upon the Egyptians. This formidable Egyptian god connects with Nebo because writing, astronomy, mathematics, and botany are attributed to the three powerful gods Nebo, Thoth, and Hermes. Three separate deities or just one? They all are associated with each other and their attributes are identical.

Some believe Thoth was the architect of Stonehenge because he taught the Egyptians the art of building. If Thoth was not the driving force of this vast edifice then who was? Someone must have been the designer and instigator of such an enormous enterprise, and the many others like it. This awe-inspiring, ibis-headed god knew the secrets of the heavens, which he inscribed in sacred books that are purportedly buried in a tomb in Memphis. However, it is quite possible that these books ended up secreted in Solomon's Temple, and consequently sought by the Knights Templar, amongst others. Thoth was also the Moon God, Lord of the Eight, and god of sciences. Such was Thoth's power that after he succeeded Horus to the throne of Egypt he reigned for over three thousand years.

In the cosmos, the many love affairs of the gods are their entrances of planets into the houses of the zodiac, but on earth, they relate to history. The gods duplicated themselves, and just as Eve was said to have been part of Adam, so it was with all the wives of the gods, with the exception of Ishtar who was a goddess in her own right.

The great triad of Babylonian goddesses was Ishtar/Venus, Anat the heaven goddess, and Asherah the earth goddess. Ishtar is the morning star and the goddess of war, but at night, the goddess of love. Beautiful, demanding, and capricious, she was the lover of gods and mortals alike. This daughter of Enlil rejoices in the catchy title The Whore Who Sits on the Throne of the Seas. She was also Hebe/Subat, the barmaid of the gods. Worshipped in many nations and known by numerous names, in Sumer, she was Ishtar; in Canaan Ashtarte; in Moab Ashtar; in Mesopotamia Attar; in southern Arabia Athtar; in Syria Atargatis; and in Greece she was Ashtarte. She wielded enormous influence over a widespread area and diverse cultures. Remnants of her power are visible today in numerous ideograms worldwide, and her impact is seemingly undiminished.

Ishtar, to the Egyptians is Isis, Queen of Heaven, who goes in search of her lover Osiris, God the Father, and, miraculously briefly restores him to life. Impregnated by him, she bears a son, Horus, the son of god. Each new king, as an incarnation of Horus, was venerated as the new morning star Venus. Upon his death, he merged with Osiris to ascend to the stars. In ancient scripts, the gods seem to have been actual mortals— duality of god-kings, as were the pharaohs.

Scores of myths and legends recount the recurring themes of death and resurrection, demonstrated particularly by the love affairs of the various gods and goddesses. One of the stories concerns Ishtar and her lover Tammuz. She was so angry with him for raping his sister that she dispatched him to the underworld. Repenting, she went in search of him and remained there for three days and three nights as a corpse. Enki/Ea, lord of the earth, takes pity on her, and restores her to life by giving her revitalizing food and water, but Tammuz was consigned to spending half the year in the underworld. Yet again, Ishtar, in her role as Belit, the wife of the mighty Bel, goes to the underworld to find her lord to restore him to his House of Taurus as Tau the Bull where he will repeat the zodiacal cycle again. As goddess, wife, mistress, and lover she plays many roles, and the number of myths surrounding this impressive goddess are inexhaustible, as seemingly she was herself! How was it possible for Ishtar to be Sargon's lover and the protectress she undoubtedly was? Was this beauty immortal, or a re-occurring reincarnation? Possibly the virgin, who was required to become a prostitute of the temple of Ishtar for one year, assumed the role of this goddess. If the holy marriage enacted in the raised sanctuary of the ziggurat by the high priestess and the king brought forth a son, should the stars foretell it, he would become the sacred king. Various forms of the natural world were sacred to Ishtar. Sometimes as the goddess Derceto, she was a mermaid: a woman to the hips with the tail of a fish. As Aphrodite, the cypress tree was her symbol of everlasting life because trees generally were sacred emblems. The pomegranate was Ishtar's special fruit with its thousands of seeds signifying fertility, and her peculiar bird was the dove. Ishtar's two female attendants were goddesses: Demeter the earth and Hecate the moon, who, with Ishtar as Venus, formed a trinity. Ishtar is easily remembered today by the name bestowed upon her by the Saxons: Eastre, after Astrae, the queen of heaven of all the stars. Ishtar's Gate in Babylon, covered with blue tiles, represented the other gods of that city, principally Marduk and Adad. One of the museums in modern Berlin displays a replica of the Gate of Ishtar.

Her influence has permeated many cultures throughout the centuries, and her emblems and symbols of power can been recognized in extraordinary places, the Vatican being a prime example. As Venus, her symbol of the eight-pointed star decorates the windows of the papal palace.

The second goddess of the triad was Anat, Anu's wife and therefore the heaven goddess whom the Amurru worshiped at Salem before the advent of the Israelites. Anat was a militant goddess who had the misfortune of falling in love with a mortal, Adonai. This so enraged her brother Tammuz that he caused fires to ravage the lands, making them infertile. To save his people, Adonai offered his life by stabbing himself. Many mourned his death, especially the women who lusted after him, so Tammuz relented. As a lasting memorial to Adonai, he caused Adonai's blood to flow from the mountain each spring where the fields were awash with blood red poppies. In this manner, Adonai was resurrected. The concept of self-sacrifice and resurrection was of paramount importance to the ancients.

Asherah, the third in the triad of goddesses, sprang from the head of Zeus. She was the Earth Mother who is exalted in Pisces, and is the consort of Yahweh. Asherah had many names: Esharra, Mother Earth, Hera to the Greeks—She Who Walks on the Sea. She was the Mother of the Heraclidae. From Hera, Hurepa—Europe—is derived. She becomes Niobe who denies the power of Lat and is doomed, turning to stone. There is a rock on Mount Sipylus that resembles a woman thought to be Niobe who is a symbol for grief.

Zeus first appears as Zius Udra, spirit of the sun in Pisces. He was born where no man casts a shadow—possibly at Syrene, Mount Aswan, because in the summer solstice, the sun is vertically overhead, casting no shadow. In the zodiac, this is the House of Cancer where Zeus is exalted. Persians regarded Zeus as the whole of circle of heaven, making sacrifices to him on mountaintops. Zeus is Dis; Dios is Theos. He is also Jupiter and Bel.

Flood myths abound throughout India and Greece, and many versions are recounted, such as in the *Epic of Gilgamesh* and the story of Enki and Ea. Enki was the Sumerian water god who corresponds with Ea. In some myths, Enki was the one who advised the building of a boat to save humankind from the wrath of Enlil. Being overwhelmed and irritated by the perpetual noise and clamor of humanity, he sent a great flood to destroy the world. Warnings by various deities bore the same message of impending doom: build a boat, take refuge, and hide the wisdom of the ages. The Greeks thought Aquarius was the instigator of the great flood, but the flood legend concerning Noah comes from the original Babylonia. Noah is associated with both Nebo and Hermes. Berosus, the Chaldean historian and Babylonian priest, studied the signs and projected a cataclysmic "end of the world." Thereupon Chronus instructed Noah to build a vessel to protect him from the impending flood, and enjoined Berosus to write a history of the beginning, procedure, and conclusion of all things, and to bury these annals in the city of the sun at Sippara.

After the subsidence of the flood, Noah's sons, who correspond to the various gods, established critical boundaries. Japheth, who is Bel (Zeus/Jupiter), had the area of the western side of the zodiac. Ham, or Nergal (Ares/Mars), the Winged Lion, ruled Neter Ta, Egypt, and the underworld south of the zodiac. Shem is Ninib/Saturn, whose sphere of influence was the eastern part of the zodiac, the last to appear in the zodiac, the seventh planet, Resh. This is the great god and lord of heaven, lord of might in the midst of the divine circle.

The lives, love affairs, and wars of the deities directly affected the mortals who fell under their jurisdiction. Ilanu and Ishtarate referred to the whole pantheon of gods. The name for the unseen gods was Ilu, Akkadian for Lofty Ones, and the Semitic El. The gods made distinctions with the souls of the departed: heroes were welcomed in a fertile sunlit island separated from mortals by the impassable river of death that leads to the abode of Allat, the dreadful queen of the underworld. The tree of life and the spring of life flourished in this land. This region was first placed in the center of the marshes of the Euphrates where it flowed into the Gulf, but eventually it was transferred north to such a great distance that it tended to disappear. Known as the Garden of Hera, it may have been the lost Atlantis.

God, unique, omnipotent and omnipresent was known as The Eternal One or The Solitary One, and venerated as the center of all light and

27

energy. Alalu was the king in heaven before Anu succeeded him, and Al was the first word used for God although many names were given to him depending on the culture and their perception of the Divine One: Adonai, Allah, Anu, Aum, Braam, Deus, El, Elohim, Jah, Jehovah, Sol, Vishnu, Yu-el, and Yahweh. All are names for God.

Yahweh, I am that I am, was the son of El who dwelt at the sources of the two rivers the Tigris and the Euphrates in the midst of two streams, the Two Deeps, the Black and Caspian Seas. In Kabbalah (the hidden teachings of the Essenes, a monastic Jewish cult of the Qumran community), the first principle is the name of the deity, existence is existence, that is I am who is Kether.

In Sumer's distant past, humanity's first golden age, they worshipped a single deity, Enlil, a son of Anu, lord of the wind; however, with the arrival of Enki and other gods, jealousies and rivalries abounded. The Amorites called Enlil Adonai Zedec, which translates as Lord of Justice, a link with Melchizedek. His story compares to that of Bel's as Jupiter and Melchizedek. The spirit of the word is Enlil; the spirit of the heart of Anu is Enlil. Enlil is also the earth, and in heaven becomes the planet Jupiter. He was a great benefactor of humankind who established peace and prosperity, teaching the use of the pickaxe and the plough. Enlil executes the will of Anu and guarantees order against chaos. He is the protector of the Tablets of Destiny and so can command the fate of all things. However, he has within himself the powers of destruction, and committed grave sins for which the other gods banished him to Hades. Enlil was the father of the gods and one of the rulers of the Annunaki.

The Annunaki, who appear in the *Enuma Elish*, were the high council of the gods. They were deities of both the Sumerians and the Akkadians. Sumerians firmly believed in their existence, and by referring to them in myriad ways, give us a vivid description of the influence of the Annunaki, the children of Anu, their king. Their name meant "heaven came to earth; and they were often referred to as the Lofty Ones. This assembly of gods was responsible for meting out justice, which they determined by means of a voting system. They appointed the kings, and according to the Sumerian king list, which was compiled around 2000 BC, "kingship was lowered from heaven." This list provides us with a complete record of the monarchs from the beginning. The princely race of the Annunaki constructed reservoirs and developed agricultural systems with water irrigation channels. They also built great edifices that the Romans may very well have copied in building their aqueducts for which they are famous. The Annunaki were the highest ranks of the gods on earth, and their home was reputed to be Dilmun, an area in the Persian Gulf. Dilmun, of ancient legend, became a veritable paradise when Utu, the sun god, filled it with water, as the water god Enki commanded. Dilmun was a pure, bright land knowing neither sickness nor death. Many believe that the Annunaki slept with mortal women thus making their offspring half mortal and half divine. Their descendants are endowed with supernatural gifts: second sight; the ability to predict the future; the casting of horoscopes; levitation and out-of-body experiences. These abilities have been well documented through the ages and continue to confound us. Shakespeare said it well: – "There are more things in heaven and earth {Horatio} than are dreamt of in your philosophy."

The gods had their own earthly dwelling places. Eridu was the first city of the gods, and both Ea and Enki laid claim to it. Built near the head of the Persian Gulf, it was the city of the first Sumerian kingships. Adapa, (Adam, primeval man) was placed in charge of the temple of Enki. The first priest, he introduced the worship of the gods and supposedly ascended to heaven. Sacred Erech belonged to Anu.

The Egyptians gods bear such similarity to those of Sumer and Babylonia that it may have been simply an adjustment of language and culture. For example, the links between Ra/Sun/Shamash, Shu/Air/ Scorpio, Tefnut/Water/Aquarius, and Geb/Earth/Taurus as the four cherubim are immediately recognizable. Osiris was God the Father as were other gods. Isis shared the title of the Queen of Heaven with Ishtar. The heavenly twins were Shu and Tefnut—Gemini.

Are their gods, the Neteru, actually the Annunaki? The description of the divine land of the gods—Ta-Neteru is virtually word for word that of the Fields of Aalu (House of El) quoted elsewhere. In the legend of the Destruction of Mankind found in the tomb of Seti I, Ra became tired of ruling disobedient children on earth and retired to the sky, reminding us of that legend about Anu forsaking the world to find some peace and quiet. When Ra had reached the upper regions, he inspected the territory he had chosen for his own, declared his purpose of gathering many around him in it, and created for their future accommodation, the various divisions of the heavenly world. Ra proclaimed, "Let there be set a great field," and there appeared a field of rest. "I will gather in it plants," and there appeared the Field of Aarun (Aalu). "Therein do I gather as its inhabitants things which hang from heaven, even the stars." This was the Elysian Fields, the House of El, surrounded by a wall of iron broken by several doors and crossed by a river. The ways leading to it were mysterious indeed. *The Book of the Dead* speaks of it as "the fields which produce the divine harvest," where the blessed spent their time harvesting the barley, which apparently grew to the astonishing height of seven cubits (an ancient measure approximately the length of a forearm). It was to this part of the divine world that souls made their way on the death of the body.

The stories of creation and the roles played by gods and mortals intertwine. Not only does the enormous influence of the zodiacal circle mark the boundaries of these gods, but it also weaves together their legends. Perceived through the eyes of the different cultures, the encompassing circle of worship and rituals draws all together in diverse ways.

The Sumerians believed that the beings were immortal, anthropomorphic and blessed with divine powers. They assumed that the creation of humans was solely for serving these beings, as indeed the deities themselves were convinced.

Habitations of the gods were the mountains and highlands in western Asia: Scythia, regarded as the summit of the earth's surface. This was the blessed place of peace and light where splendor reigned forever, and where war and death were unknown.

Similarities between the literature of the Sumerians and the Bible are evident. The roles of the gods and priest-kings were interwoven in the tapestry of life since the earliest days of man's history. The Sumerians influenced many peoples and cultures that preceded the Hebrews, notably the Babylonians and the Hurrians, who passed their legends down through the nomadic tribes.

The names Adam and Eve have an intriguing history too, linking together the three foremost religions of Judaism, Christianity, and Islam. Adam in the Koran is given as a race not a man. Adam as the first man is the House of Aries (Asia Minor) and a remnant of Cro-Magnon, Aurignacians, and Amurru. In Hebrew, Adam translates as red earth. Referred to as the Lady Hurri of the Hurrian race, Eve had many names and played numerous roles. She was the consort of Adad, the storm god who rules the House of Aries, which was one of the original lands of the Amurru, whose boundaries extended from Babylon through to Thrace. Eve is also Asherah or Hera, the wife of Zeus.

For the ancient Persians, Zoroaster was a powerful influence and a great religious reformer. He is said to have lived around 1200 BC; he was the founder of Zurvanism, and was known as He Who Possesses the Secret Formula, sharing this title with Thoth. Zoroaster denounced all the old gods and preached that Ahura Mazda was the creator god and the one true god of goodness and light. The symbol for Ahura Mazda was an arc over his head bearing the twelve signs of the zodiac. He was in conflict with his twin Angra Mainyu who represented darkness and evil. Angra Mainyu is depicted as a winged deity having the body of a man with the head of a lion. Zoroastrians venerated fire, another symbol of Ahura Mazda, and they had faith that angels kept constant watch over all, their creed preserved by the Magi.

Libra/Themis identifies with Ma'at, the goddess of truth, justice, and order, both moral and physical. Portrayed wearing a feather of truth on her head and a bandage covering her eyes, she is a symbol of blind justice. She decided the fate of souls by weighing their lives in the balance as did Thoth. The word Ma'at translates in the annals of Freemasonry as embodying the concept of their whole attitude to life— knowledge and truth. These concepts also were essential to the lives of the Druids, who held the belief that the soul passes from one person to another at the time of death.

Consider now other words that have their origin in the old religion. The Phoenician word *sydyk* meaning the just and *zedec*, Lord of All Seven *khabirim*, is very close to the modern word zodiac. Zedec is god of the night sky and in Kabbalah stands for Jupiter. The various spellings may have different meanings, but all make connections to the zodiac. Zedec (*Tsedeq*) is one of the two pillars of the Temple of Jerusalem (the other is Mishpat). Zaddik is righteousness. Zaddik priests were teachers of Kabbalah. Sydyk is also Zeus/Bel.

The language spoken in parts of Europe is Gaelic, pronounced Gallic. Gal is circle. Kerche or kirk, the Scottish word for church, means Her Place, that of Circe the goddess of the circle. Kirks were stone circles used for worship. Most thickly found in Palestine, the Edomites (the Amurru) used them, and these sons of Adam were the only people mentioned as having used stone circles for this purpose. The churches of the Knights Templar also were of this design. Curetes, companions of the sacred kings, young men who shaved their heads, were the priest-assistants of the worshippers of Bel, lord of the earth. The word Alleluia stems from the Aramaic AL-LALA, hail to the god of heaven. Altar is Al—God and Tau—cross. The Greek Tau or Semitic Taw, the last letter of the Hebrew Alphabet, meaning mark in its early form, was an *X*, and the Phoenicians always carried this symbol.

Dragons and dragon slayers, too, are a recurring theme in folklore and mythology holding a persistent fascination. Ninurta, the son of Enlil and Sud (Ninkharsag), slays Asag the monster who dwells in Kur, the nether world. Curiously, Kur, originally thought of as cosmic space, is a thread linking Ninurta and Bel, both of whom overcome Ti'amat. Kur also translates as place or house.

In the epic story *Gilgamesh*, the great sun of the zodiac slays the dragon Huwawa. One must know the zodiac to understand fully the verses of the *Epic of Gilgamesh*. It tells of the sun's journey around the zodiac to end in the House of Pisces, which, as the sun reappears here to begin the journey again, heralds the rebirth of the earth, giving the promise of eternal life. The circle is 360 degrees, while the year's length is 364 and half days, so for the odd days the sun must disappear. Gilgamesh accomplishes this by sleeping until he accepts the bread of life. Consisting of twelve songs, the Babylonians referred to this epic as the Gilgamesh Cycle. It influenced the early Semitic religion, and the final epic was a Semitic creation clearly indicating their connection with the zodiacal religion and methods of worship.

Celtic mythology contains many allegorical stories stemming from zodiacal influence. Celtic Europe stretched from Asia Minor through France and Spain to the northernmost isles of Great Britain. The stories of heroic combat and the quest for the grail have entranced us for centuries. Nennius found the earliest records of King Arthur in ancient Britain in Welsh history. Arthur was one of the nine heroes of the world who drew the fabled enchanted sword Excalibur from the stone, establishing his right to kingship. The legend of his conception—his mother lying with a man with magical powers—harkens back to many previously-recorded stories of gods and their love affairs with mortal women. King Arthur is closely associated with the zodiac, as is Hercules, many believing that both the legends describe their journeys on its path. Some of Arthur's knights and indeed his queen, Guinevere, have a connection with the zodiac; for instance: Gawain in Aries; Ector in Taurus; Lohot in Gemini; Lancelot in Leo; Guinevere in Virgo; Mordred in Scorpio Arthur portrayed on his horse in Sagittarius; and Perceval in Aquarius and Pisces.

Arthur was Arcturus, Athur, Anahit, and because his emblem was the bear, he was associated with the constellation Ursa Major. As Athur, he has no place in heaven because he is the god of artificial irrigation canals, which make him simply an earthly deity.

Arthur of Britain was a warrior king immortalized in legend and poetry. The English call Ursa Major the Great Bear. Possibly the creation of the Round Table was inspired by the circular motion of Ursa Major. The original Round Table of Uther Pendragon held one hundred and fifty knights. A round table hangs in a great hall in Winchester, England, which some maintain is the original, and although difficult to prove, it is, nevertheless, a very romantic tradition.

The grail, said to have been brought to Britain by Joseph of Arimathea, had a special place reserved for it at the Round Table. The grail appeared to the knights amid a dazzling white radiance, and was esteemed as a source of spiritual nourishment, health, and plenty. Subsequently it disappeared. The Knights of the Round Table are famous not only for romantic love, chivalry, and charity, but more importantly for their quest for the grail. Sir Galahad, the pure and perfect knight, purportedly found it because Joseph granted him the blessing of holding the chalice before he died. The Round Table, symbolizing wholeness and unity, commemorated the table of the Last Supper, forming the link between Christianity and the religion of the zodiac. Merlin himself was a Christian, and although blessed with magical powers, fell prey to the snares of lovely women. The romances, a rich source for inspiration, rest on the pagan foundation cycle of seasons—the circle of the zodiac and the concept of rebirth.

Upon his death, Arthur was borne away by three queens, the three goddesses Asherah, Ishtar, and Anat. The queens took Arthur to enchanted Avalon to tend his wounds and to guard him until that time he might return, "When Britain needs him." The supposed graves of Arthur and his queen Guinevere are at Glastonbury, which is identified with Avalon. The inscription on Arthur's grave reads, "Here lies Arthur, king that was, king that shall be." Joseph of Arimathea planted his staff at Glastonbury, forming the Holy Thorn Tree, which blossomed every year on the anniversary of Christ's birth. Although the tree was destroyed, its descendants flower at Christmas when one of its sprigs is given to the British monarch.

The chalice that bore the very life-blood of Christ holds the highest reverence of all. Christianity really began with St. Peter taking the holy cup from Jerusalem to Rome. It has a long history, and at times was lost, which perhaps led to the quest for the Holy Grail. These words derive from Sang Real, Blood Royal. The search for the spiritual food and drink of eternal life promising immortality has long been a quest of humankind. Conceivably, this mystery reverts to the legends of the gods in search for Sa, the essence of life, which carried with it health, vigor, and life. Sa was a magic fluid that the gods could transmit to humankind. The soul receives Sa at birth and at that moment, the stars determine its fate below.

The tarot cards and the grail interweave with the zodiacal journey of the sun. Those who have the ancient knowledge can tell one's destiny by using the cards. Each of the pictures represents various gods and goddesses of the pagan religion. The trumps (triumph) centered on the story of a sacred king, associating with Ishtar and her lover Tammuz who disappeared into the Underworld.

Countless locations around the world have mystical legends that are intriguing because of their inexplicable links to the zodiac, one of which concerns a church in England, the Priory at Christchurch. The memorial garden of the priory has beautifully wrought iron gates depicting the signs of the zodiac. This splendid church is the possessor of a miraculous beam for which it is renowned, and the account of its acquisition is remarkable. During the construction of the church, there was some confusion as to the exact position of the foundations, because originally the plans called for them to be about a mile away from its present location. The masons laid the stones according to plan, but when they returned the next morning; astoundingly the stones had been moved. After occurring a few times, the master mason eventually decided to keep them where they had been re-sited, taking it to be divine guidance. A stranger appeared offering help with the construction of the church, never staying for meals or accepting payment. One evening, a beam for the roof, found to be too short, was left aside overnight by the builders. Upon their return the following morning, they were amazed to find it not only long enough, but also in its proper place. The stranger was not seen again, and they all agreed that the mysterious man must have been the Carpenter from Nazareth, so they called the priory Christchurch, eventually becoming the name of the town as well. The mystery is why such a sacred place has zodiacal gates to its memorial garden.

Another mystery concerns the glorious cathedral of Chartres. Among its many beautiful stained glass windows there are twelve depicting the signs of the zodiac and the labors of each month. This is yet another example of the inclusion of the zodiac on Christian sites, clearly demonstrating its impact on humankind throughout the ages.

Beliefs and Rituals

Splendid Serpent of the Shining Eyes is such a magnificent title! This belonged to the wondrous Enlil; Sumerian lord of the wind, whose consort Ninkharsag was the Serpent Lady. Serpent mythology is widespread and the focus of many cults throughout history. After thousands of years, the serpent remains a source of fascination. Beginning with the ancient tribes around the Persian Gulf, the Heracleopolitan Dynasties of the Amurru, Kassites, Hurri, and for the peoples of the Americas, the cult worship of the serpent takes many guises. What is the attraction of the serpent and why is it so intriguing?

The earth spirit, the magnetic natural channels of energy moving under the earth, sometimes is referred to as the serpent current. The movements of the heavenly bodies modify the force of these currents. Comprehension of these movements was of paramount importance to not only the Ancients, but to people throughout the ages. Some of the stupendous earthworks, visible only from the air, and still defying explanation of their development, depict winding serpents. These occur on varied landscapes throughout the world. One of which, found in Ohio, is attributed to the ancient Native Americans. Mesoamerican cultures focus on the serpent: Quetzalcoatl—quetzal-feathered serpent— was patron of the Calmecac, the school of priestly learning and a teacher of the arts. Cihuacoatl was the serpent woman. Gucumatz, creator god of the Popul Vuh was the Serpent with the Green Feathers.

Pre-dynastic serpents represent water and rivers. The two great

36

rivers, the Tigris and Euphrates, were the two serpents of Nebo the Winged Man of Aquarius, the House of Eternal Life. A wand with two encircling serpents is the symbol for Hermes the winged man, the wings on his heels giving him the ability to move through space.

The serpent is the embodiment of wisdom, knowing the secrets of the cosmos, and holding the sacred knowledge of the gods. It betrayed this knowledge to humankind through Eve in the Garden of Eden. Eve, in common with Ishtar, also claims the dubious distinction of being The Whore who sits on the Throne of the Seas. Eden or E.Din was the abode of the righteous ones and is in the first house of Adam. As the symbol for creative energy, the serpent sheds its old skin, renewing it each year to reinforce the concept of renewal and regeneration. The serpent twines its tail around them, linking the legends for eternity.

Representing the path of the sun the serpent symbolizes eternal life in the zodiac. It is an allegorical pilgrimage starting in Aquarius and ending in Capricorn, where, with its tail in its mouth it represents infinity - all-in-all. In this house, it is the Serpent of Saturn. The foremost goddesses associated with the serpent cult are Ninkharsag who was reputed to be the mother of the gods, connected with creation and birth; and Hebe the goddess of the Serpent Mountain. Heracles received Hebe as his bride among the immortals, and in this instance the Romans, who believed she had the power to restore youth, called her Juventas—Youth.

However, the serpent also represents chaos—Zu/Tia'mat slain by Marduk is symbolic of both wisdom and chaos, and the focus of the phallic cults. The serpent was the totem of the Amurru, princes of Serpent Mountain, who built the great stone giant in England, he of the raised phallus, undisputedly a symbol for their phallic cult.

The Canaanites worshipped the snake god Basilisk, a phallic god, from which derives the term basilica. Curiously, this is a type of church, the most famous being the Basilica of St. Peter in Rome.

Le Serpent Rouge refers to a ground plan of St. Sulpice in Paris that has chapels devoted to various saints. Certain texts discovered there consist of thirteen short poems, twelve corresponding to the signs of the zodiac, with the thirteenth referring to the serpent holder.

Capturing our imagination, legends teem with serpents and dragons.

Demonstrating the power given to him by God, Moses threw his staff upon the ground before the Pharaoh, which turned into a snake and slithered across the palace floor astounding the onlookers. When it transformed back into his staff, it further mystified them. Active only once a year, the Oracle at Delphi was insufficient to encourage and comfort the populace, so Apollo spears the serpent to energize it. In an age-old Danish custom, an adder is buried beneath the threshold of their houses to ward off evil spirits. In Ireland, where St. Patrick cleared the country of snakes, the people sang the saint's praises seeking protection from the devil.

A vine/serpent coils around the pillar Boaz, a single pillar in Rosslyn Chapel. This is immensely significant because this symbol links the zodiac to the Freemasons. For the Ritual of the Twenty-First Degree of the Freemasons, the story of the shrine to Bel, the Tower of Babel is related tying in directly to the ancient religion. This chapel abounding with myriad references to many cults and religious artifacts is a highly visible connection between the Freemasons, Cistercians, and the Knights Templar. They based their rituals and beliefs upon the Jerusalem Church, of which James the Just was the priestly messiah.

Our ancestors were vitally concerned with the effects of nature and the gods who represented the various aspects of both the natural world and the cosmos. They sought to communicate with the gods whom they believed would actively participate in their daily life and fortunes. Rituals were essential to perpetuate the worship of the deity, particular to a season or event. Passed down through the centuries, elaborate rites reflect this harmony between nature and the gods.

The Templars believed in one God, Almighty Being, venerating Melchizedek as the image of the Almighty. This concept encompassed Christian, Jew, and Muslim alike, nurturing Kabbalah and Hermes Trismegistus. The Knights Templar, more priests than knights, held all property in common. Said to hold the key to the divine secrets and true knowledge, they influenced the romances of the Round Table of King Arthur, interweaving them indelibly with the zodiac.

Priests wielded enormous power and were the true priest-kings, because only through them could approach be made to a greater god.

The main college for the priesthood was at Bethel (House of God.) Hierarch (Hi'a r'Ark) meaning priest or steward of the sacred rites stems from the Greek Hiero, which translated is priestly, holy, and sacred. Ezekiel, prophet and chief priest of the Temple of Yahweh, established the rules of the priesthood. He envisioned Yahweh's return by entering his house through Tsedeq, the Gate of Righteousness.

The priesthood associated with the religion of the zodiac provides many names, one of which is Azariah. He was a chief priest of the house of Zadok, high priest of Jerusalem and ruler of the house of God. In Hebrew Zadok translates as The Just, a title given to many. One of the curious rules of the Zadokites impelled them to marry a virgin of Israelite birth.

Rituals have always been of critical importance to the emotional security and survival of humankind, because the possibility of life after death has sparked our imagination as we seek to cling to life and yearn for life eternal. In the journey around the zodiac souls must pass through the House of Pisces, the House of Death and Resurrection to be "washed as white as snow" before "passing over the bridge" to Aries to commence their journey around the zodiac once more. The rituals of the Passover of the Lord were very precise and full instructions given (Exodus 12). Jesus was executed on the eve of Passover. The Age of Pisces fittingly began at the time of Christ. During the period before Passover, all normal activity was suspended. When the sun dawned on the horizon and Hadis had risen from the underworld, there was great rejoicing. Called *hilaria* by the Romans, possibly stemming from hail *ares*, this heralded the spring. Aries is the first House of the zodiac, marking the annual rebirth of the natural world.

The Egyptians had faith, although not in immortality, in reincarnation. They relied upon the weighing of the soul by their god Thoth. In his role of He Who Balances, he judged as to whether the soul balanced exactly with Ma'at, the goddess of truth. The scales of Libra represent not only the scales of justice, but of the balance between good and evil.

Legends abound about gods and mortals who expressed the desire of revival or reincarnation and immortality. In the *Epic of Gilgamesh*, a descendant of the immortal Utnapishtim, the hero, goes to the mountain of Mashu where the sun sets and the underworld begins, searching for the means of achieving immortality. His brother Enkidu, who was a wild man with shaggy hair, accompanied Gilgamesh. The name Enkidu stems from *en*—heaven, *ki*—earth, and *du*—move. Gilgamesh and Enkidu are the twins—Gemini.

Interweaving the pantheons of the gods of Sumer, Canaan, and Babylonia stories inevitably merge. The Sumerians influenced the Egyptians, for whom the ritual of symbolic death and resurrection was crucial to their existence. Initiates to the Order of Freemasons continue to enact this rite. The symbolic death of self to the resurrection of a newborn, sin-purged persona prepares that person for the mysteries of the Order. Their doctrines of the resurrection of the body and immortality of the soul perpetuate the beliefs and rituals of the ancients. This ritual of death and resurrection is continued and practiced in countless ways into perpetuity.

Quite a number of gods and goddesses went to the underworld for some reason or another. Most returned to continue the cycle of nature and their journey around the zodiac. The first of the gods to die and to be reborn was Bel. The *Texts of Ugarit* tell us that Bel is at the mercy of Nergal, the sun of death, and must fight Yamm, the sea god who symbolized chaos. Although Bel overcomes Yamm, he nevertheless is banished to the underworld where he languishes for the three odd days of the Babylonian year. The goddess Rhea, whom he marries in a subterranean cavern, frees him. Bel rises again as the young bull, ready to assume the many roles he plays on his journey around the zodiac yet again.

The goddess of the circle is Circe, a daughter of the sun and sister to Parsiphae, the goddess of Pisces. Circe heralds the seasons of spring and autumn, and she too will be taken to the dark underworld where Bel rules as Hades. The earth will die until her constellation reappears and life will be renewed. But of all the gods to die and to be resurrected, Nebo was the most significant. He represents Man in the zodiac. He is the symbol of creation, the intellect, the body, and the renewal of life. As the ruler of Aquarius, Nebo is ordained to die in the House of Pisces in the manner of the sacred kings. Regarded as the personification of the

40

god, he must be purified, as all must be who "pass over the bridge."

In the beginning, places of worship were groves, but to practice their rituals and enforce their beliefs, people eventually built temples and ziggurats to pay homage to their deities. The largest ziggurat was that of Bel in Babylon. The great temple was designed to resemble earth, rising like a pyramid above the city. In a series of eight stories, it had divisions of glowing colors, with a shrine of blue-glazed tile that boasted a gold dome, shimmering in the hot sun. Trees planted on the terraces provided drainage. The sanctuary standing on the highest of these levels was furnished with a great bed for the use of the god. No image stood there, and no mortal passed the night within its walls, with the exception of a single woman whom the god chose from all the women of Babylon. The priests pronounced that the deity himself came to the great bed, and the woman who became his consort thereafter was denied intercourse with a mortal man. The king embodied the local god. This ziggurat had a triple gate. Was this the Tower of Babel? Babel is Sumerian for god-gate.

Worshippers of the deities gathered at central, highly visible locations, one of the most famous being Stonehenge, the sacred site for the Druids to this day. The Druids, who appeared at the time of the great Kaldi, were priests of the Celtic nations, and were regarded as wizards. In Greek annals, mention is made of the Dryads who danced around oak trees, inhabited by a deity. The Druids are descended from the Heraclidae because they were from the tribe of Danaans, the Tidanu of Lebanon of the Dinaric race, although there is very little evidence of where the Druids actually originated.

Druids venerated mistletoe, and used golden sickles to cut it because it grew on oak trees that were sacred to Bel. On the Isle of Man in Great Britain, on the first day of May, Druids continue to celebrate the anniversary of Ba'al/Bel with the lighting of fires, and in Ireland, similar fires are kindled in Bel's name. Around 300 BC the Druids worshipped the gods Belinus/Bel, Belisama/Belit, Belatucador, Ceres, Lud and Maponus. They revered the sun Shamash/Shamus and the moon Sin/ Sean. Their aims included development of the mind, cultivation of intuition, keen observation, retentive memory, and the veneration of the truth, which mirrored the aspirations of the Persians. The Druids held the belief that at death, the soul passes from one person to another.

Certain areas in ancient Mesopotamia where the gods and mortals resided were sacred. Scythia was such a place, due to a mysterious sanctity protecting its inhabitants. It was not necessary for them to carry arms, and it was here they settled disputes. All could seek sanctuary in Scythia. The tribes here engaged in magic, and venerated the wild white horses, and they practiced the cult of the serpent. The Scythians fiercely protected their land because the rivers provided the finest and most abundant pastures and the richest supplies of fish. The Scythians worshipped few gods: Hestia (the hearth goddess), Zeus, and Earth. Apollo, Celestial Aphrodite, Heracles, and Ares were deities of secondary importance. The worship of Heracles and the value placed upon their white horses connects them with the Heraclids who were so influential in the spreading of the zodiacal religion and rituals.

Mithras, originally a sun god of the Persians, whose attributes closely resembled those of Bel, was acknowledged as the creator of the cosmos. Between 2000 and 1500 BC, he was a premier deity of the Hittites. A bronze image depicts Mithra emerging from an egg shaped zodiac ring. His initiates danced around representations of this god in the middle of a circle, with twelve dancers representing the zodiac.

Dancing is a joyous, expressive method of worship and celebration of life. The circle was the earliest dance formation, and folklore tells of how the fairies dance in enchanted circles. The frenzied dancing and the billowing garments of the Whirling Dervishes of Turkey represent the circles and motions of the cosmos.

Such is the mesmerizing mystique of the circle.

The Cross and Other Symbols

Symbols are a means for humans to transmit abstract ideas and to trigger emotional responses. They were the earliest expressions of thought and religious practices, providing communication. Buildings, edifices, vestments, and artifacts vividly depict the connections between paganism and other faiths. Maintained across the centuries, these symbols convey the powerful influence wielded by the zodiacal deities. For instance, one cannot help but wonder why such a bastion of the Christian faith as the Vatican portrays symbols of Ishtar and Shamash. So many ideograms link the cultures and intertwine the religions of the world. A good example is the Seal of Solomon, which is also the Star of David. His seal is a pentagram, which the Sumerians used as early as 4000 BC.

The seal, a six-pointed star, was a powerful talisman, because Solomon was renowned not only for his wisdom, but also for his exertion of supernatural powers, and he was rich beyond the dreams of avarice. His seal portrays the four elements, which when combined with the triangle, results in the sacred number seven.

The Phoenicians, Canaanites, Chaldeans, Sons of Anak, and the Persians carried the Tau cross. One of the earliest religious symbols, this was used far back in the prehistoric Samothracian rites. The Greek Tau or Semitic Taw in its early form was an *X*. The cross was a compass, a magnetized needle floating crosswise on water on a reed or wood, symbolizing earth, fire, water, and air, the four cherubim, and the four astral gods.

The Tau cross is possibly the three crosses that represent the trinity of body, soul, and spirit (the three crosses of Calvary.) The Triple Tau was the Temple of Jerusalem, the Holy of Holies, and the Temple of Yahweh. For the Gnostics, the cross symbolized the two worlds of earth and the cosmos, and in geographical terms used the Tau as a marker to divide the lands above the equator and those beneath. St Anthony was crucified upon a Tau cross, which later became a symbol for one of the earliest Orders of the Knights Templar. A serpent entwined around a Tau cross is another major symbol for the Templars. Considered to represent king, priest and prophet, it has been venerated throughout the centuries by a mélange of cultures and religions. The four evangelists, Matthew, Mark, Luke, and John, the writers of the first four books of the New Testament, are linked with the four points of the compass and the signs of Aquarius, Leo, Taurus, and Scorpio respectively, their symbol being associated with the fixed cross of astrologers.

Thousands of years before Christianity, the cross was an expression of adulation, and recognized as a mark of faith in South America. The cross comes in many shapes and sizes; for instance, the Egyptian cross, or ankh, symbolizes both life and eternal life. The Jerusalem cross is five crosses in one, the four smaller crosses representing the four gospels and conceivably the four cherubim—earth, air, fire, and water of the zodiac. The equal-armed cross was a symbol for Shamash the sun god, whose domain was in the center of the zodiac. A cross within a circle symbolically emphasizes the connection of heaven and earth.

The way of the cross is to perfect conduct, subdue one's lower nature, and an endeavor to find the light, which is knowledge, self-knowledge, and wisdom. The cube of Freemasonry, ashlar, a smooth cube, denoting the aspirants' own nature, becomes a cross. The Rouge-Croix blends pagan rites with the mysteries of Christianity.

The embracing circle of the Celtic cross also reflects the symbol of eternal life, and is similar to the broad Maltese cross of the Templars, signifying guardianship. Fascinatingly, the foundations of a fishing village found in Mexico form the cross of the Keltoi (Celts). This is recognized properly only when viewed from the air in common with many symbols of worship, which, unless viewed from a great height, would remain undetected. The architects of such massive marks of worship surely were gifted with tremendous powers of creativity and imagination, and one wonders if they were able ever to fully appreciate their completed work. Gods and goddesses, priest-kings, warriors, lovers, and all manner of things are represented in some way, easily recognizable for some, or meaningfully obscure to deflect the curiosity of the uninitiated. The mark of Yahweh was a crucifix motif of warriors of certain tribes who worshipped the god of war, Nergal. The Urartians protected themselves with round shields, considering them somewhat sacred, because not only did they depict the twin gods of the family tree, but additionally the figures of the zodiacal gods.

Centuries—old symbols represent both people and objects, playing a crucial role in our comprehension of the world around us. Some symbols were exclusive pictorial marks with which to identify the pantheon of gods and goddesses. Their symbols were a vital form of communication, conveying the message of power, their role in the hierarchy, and particular place in the scheme of things. Obelisks, found everywhere, are phallic symbols, and appropriately are symbolic for Nebo as god of creation, and for Ra, the supreme Egyptian sun god. Representations of respect, created in other forms, are in the signs and symbols of the alphabet, for example. Aleph is the most sacred letter of the Hebrew alphabet. Indicative of the deity, it is seldom pronounced. Aleph in Kabbalah is Air, which is timeless, and its ideogram is *OX*, the beginning and the end. The ancient Semitic religion had three primary gods: Shamash the sun, Sin the moon, and Venus, whose divine symbol was the eight-pointed star.

Symbols represented many of the deities, not only to portray their area of influence, but also to instill awe in the eye of the beholder. A combination of human and animal depicts many gods and goddesses in diverse cultures. Allat, the actual sovereign of her country, was grotesque. She was ill-formed and shaggy, with the muzzle of a lion, claws of a bird of prey, but with the body of a woman. Each of her hands is a large serpent representing rivers, and her children are two lions representing Egypt and Ethiopia. Depicted standing on the back of a horse, Allat is also Ereshkigal, the Great Earth Mother, who is queen of the underworld.

Another fearsome god is Angra Mainyu. He is a winged deity having the body of a man with the head of a lion, whose symbol is the snake. A spirit of darkness, representing evil, he is notorious for creating poverty and indolence. A god of Mithraism, he was a premier deity for the Assyrians.

The heavens have always captured our imagination as enigmatic, promoting myths, and inviting exploration and definition. The cylinder seals of the first millennium before Christ convey the myth of Atalanta, who, as the moon, is the fastest moving planet travelling on her journey around the zodiac, changing her shape each month. The golden balls associated with her represent the other planets.

The serpent plays a significant role in mythology because as the zodiacal symbol for eternal life, it represents the path of the sun. In Capricorn, where it has its tail in its mouth, it is both the Serpent of Saturn and Ouroboros, symbolizing immortality and eternity. The serpent also represents water. The two serpents of Mercury/Nebo, the Winged Man, are the rivers Tigris and Euphrates. Six thousand years ago, the Aborigines of Australia created paintings of the rainbow serpent that is central to the beliefs of these tribes. Understandably, they regarded the serpent as the source of life because they associated it with the waterways.

Mazzaloth is the Circle of the Zodiac. Masloth means twelve signs. The signs of the zodiac depict not only the attributes of the ruler of each house, but also the history of its geographical location and peoples, and analyzed, explain the mansions of the gods.

The Ram is the sign for Aries, the first house, whose mother goddess was Khumbaba, the sheep goddess. The sign for Taurus is the head and horns of a bull, because Bel, as Zeus in this house, takes the form of a bull to represent the Earth. Gemini's sign represents the heavenly twins who were Jupiter/Bel and Saturn/Ninib. The sign for Cancer is the crab. Cancer is associated with the moon and its goddess, Ishtar. Leo's ruler is Nergal; the winged lion of myth and astrology, so two rampart lions are one of the symbols for this house. Another symbol for Leo is the sun because this is the house of Shamash, when he is at his zenith. The sheaf of corn held by Virgo, the young bride, represents fertility and the harvest, and is the symbol for Anat, queen of heaven. The scales are the sign for Libra. Maat, who is easily recognizable with her eyes bandaged and holding the scales, is the goddess of truth, justice, and order, both moral and physical. Originally, Libra and Scorpio was one house whose sign was the claws of the eagle, but eventually these houses divided. In the *Epic of Gilgamesh*, the Scorpion gods of Mashu guard the entrance to the underworld. Mashu was a magic mountain forming a boundary between the houses. The house of Scorpio is in Pakistan, and the symbol is a scorpion. Sagittarius is ruled by Bel, who in this house is Samugan, the god of cattle. Enkidu, half man, half bull was the first representation so it is fitting for its sign to be the centaur with an arrow. The origin of Capricorn's interesting sign, a scythe, is due to the fact that its ruler Ninib/Chronus/Saturn is the Grim Reaper. His duty was to disperse the house of Anu. Portrayed as an old man, Ninib gathers souls in Capricorn. Aquarius is the House of the Cup, whose sign is the water bearer and/or the cup symbolizing Ea, the god of water who rules this realm. Nebo, as a later ruler of Aquarius, is the symbol for creation of the intellect and the body, the renewal of life, the life-producing fluid of which the phallus is the symbol. The house of Pisces bears the sign of the fish. Yamm is the sea god of Pisces, the House of Two Fishes.

Shamash/Helios the sun, the flaming disk of life and death, has his own sign of a lion, first seen in Aquarius. His divine symbol was the equal-armed cross, which later became the symbol for Nebo as the winged man. The sun was revered by almost every culture throughout the world, and ideograms reflect this observance of energy, power, and renewed youth.

The swastika, which for most people represents the evil and tyranny of Nazi rule, was actually first found in Sumer dating from around 3000 BC. Having a spinning design both clockwise and anti-clockwise, it is associated with the sun and the very life force, and is therefore regarded as a most positive expression of worship. This sign, in various designs, has been used not only by many cultures including the ancient Greeks, the Celts, and the Vikings, but by Christians, too, as a symbol for the Divine Being.

A square is an important piece of Masonic symbolism, with its four points of earth, air, water, and fire. Within the circle of the zodiac, these four represented four of the known planets and the four cherubim of Kabbalah: earth—Taurus, sun—Leo, air—Scorpio, and water—Aquarius. The cube of Freemasonry is a symbol of truth and stability.

In alchemy, the up and down triangles are symbols for fire and water. In Freemasonry, the triangle represents the spiritual, physical, and psychological part of a person. The triangle may have been an astrological chart at the time of King David's birth.

The hexagram is one of the oldest symbols, consisting of two overlapped triangles, and represents the traditional elements of earth, air, fire, and water. In the Hindu religion it is called the Shatkona. In oriental mysticism, the octagon within a circle is sacred.

The history of Jesus is highly coincidental with many signs and portents from the ancient religion of the zodiac. Is it simply a coincidence that the great star of Capricorn was Mah, and its goddess Rhea? The star of Bethlehem was an object in the night sky leading the magi, the hereditary priesthood, to where the new king lay. These were learned men, astrologers well versed in reading signs in the skies, who possibly used an astrolabe to foretell the conjunction of Jupiter, the king planet, with Regulus, the king star. They were able to recognize the signs of the conjunction of Jupiter, Saturn, and Mars in the constellation of Pisces at the time of the birth of Christ. Some call the constellation of Orion the Three Kings and the Babylonians referred to it as the Shepherd of Anu. Orion is depicted as fighting Taurus the bull. The actual name Orion may have derived from the Akkadian Uru-anna, the Light of Heaven.

Reeds are a very ancient symbol. Found on pieces of plaster at the Persian Gulf, they are a symbol for Virgo/Ishtar. Reeds later identified with witches as a broomstick. They were also symbols of purification in Celtic folklore. The magi, median holy men, used a bundle of besom (a kind of trefoil common in Egypt cultivated mainly for fodder) to foretell the future. When marching in procession wearing long white robes and tall felt caps with cheek pieces, they carried a bundle of reeds, essential for every sacrifice.

There is much symbolism incorporated into the building of cathedrals and temples and other artifacts. Curiously, papal vestments depict emblems of Ishtar, Ba'al and Shamash. These are just some examples of the mystery of the zodiacal influence. Indeed, the Vatican purportedly owns the largest zodiac in the world, and St Peter's Square boasts an eight-rayed sun wheel design symbolic of Ishtar. The obelisk in the center is a customary representation of Baal's organ of reproduction.

The circle, signifying eternal life, is considered by some to represent the eye of the Great Mother Goddess, known by various names according to the race. It is one of the most widely used expressions of worship. The Hopi tribe of Native Americans regards it as sacred, as do many other cultures. The word Hopi translates as peaceful people whose philosophy is that all life is a journey, with the circle representing this journey. The intricate intertwining of nature, gods, humankind, and spirits creates the harmony that for them is essential to life. The medicine wheel or sacred hoop reflects the belief of Native Americans that the Great Spirit created nature in the round. The wheel is a quadratic circle that is associated with the quadrants of the circle of the zodiac, the four cherubim, and the points of the compass.

Chartres Cathedral has a circular maze as its floor, denoting the way of truth and enlightenment, because since time immemorial, this theme conveys the message of the timeless, constant cycle of change.

The circle is a symbol for God: infinity.

Significant Numbers

Sumerian scholars relied upon mathematics for solutions not only to the complexities of the universe, but for the essentials to daily life. The priests and scribes of Babylonia and Sumer probably were the ones responsible for the development of symbolic numbers, and their fables and wisdom handed down through successive priesthoods have enriched our lives. The precision of the zodiacal circle and its exact science not only would have satisfied humanity's need for order and a pattern for their existence, but also preserved the power and mysticism of the priest-kings of the times.

The Egyptian god Thoth, the god of mathematics and astronomy (amongst his other attributes) is thought to have invented figures. Numerology is the study of the occult significance of numbers. From time immemorial, astrologers throughout the ages have shared the same beliefs. Pagans, Gnostics, Pythagoreans, Mayans, and Freemasons alike all revered the mysticism of the sacred formulae of numbers. The numbers twelve and seven are especially important, appearing repeatedly in many renowned texts including the book of Revelation in the Bible, and the Islamic Umm al-Kitab, the Mother of Books.

The Babylonians devised an assortment of dials and the division of days into hours, which is still in use. A single wedge, using the number sixty for their numerical reckoning, charted the stars to within a sixtieth of an hour. Relative to their importance in the hierarchy, a sacred number was assigned to each of the gods. The word *dis* first was applied to Anu, the supreme lord of heaven who merited the degree of sixty. Variations of *dis* gradually came into use for all the heaven gods. The sacred number for Jesus is 888, and for Mithras, 360. Enlil's number is 50, Ea's is 40, Sin's is 30, and Ishtar's is 15 to name just a few. Imitating the gods according to their merit, Freemasons are bestowed with hierarchal degrees. The mystical symbol SSS or the number 666 was the secret symbol of the ancient pagan mysteries and may represent the devil.

Throughout the centuries, numbers have been regarded as hallowed. The Wisdom of Solomon 11:20 states, "God has arranged all things in number and measure." The Gnostics, believing that numbers could express divine truth, considered the universe to be an arrangement of numbers. So if humankind was able to grasp the complexities of numbers, the riddle of cosmic behavior ultimately would be solved. The doctrines of the Sumerians, Babylonians, Medieval Christians, and Kabbalah all reflect these suppositions.

The great mathematician Pythagoras was a renowned astrologer, and his theories were the basis for the schools of pagan mysteries. His followers thought of him as semi-divine, his house constituting a sanctuary of the mysteries. An initiate of the Egyptian Mysteries, he was part scholar, priest, and magician, and reputed to be a son of Apollo (Ninib). According to Iamblichus, the Greek novelist, Pythagoras stated, "Number is the ruler of forms and ideas and the cause of gods and demons." The followers of Pythagoras were hugely interested in the relationship of symbolic numbers. Their correlation with each other and the universe, for them, was a form of worship. The seven Greek vowels represented the seven spheres of heaven. The pagan Gnostics and the Pythagoreans, in addition to the Freemasons, all regarded numbers as holy, and the sacred mathematical formulae imperative to reveal the mysteries. Geometry, revered as a noble art, was a philosophy without which the world would not turn. Architects followed geometric guidelines, believing them not only to be essential to their designs, but sacrosanct. To some, a heavenly body rules each number, and for Kabbalists each letter of the Hebrew alphabet corresponds to a number.

Expressed in numerology, the numbers one to ten are as follows:

Zero = nothing or all

One = individual, aggressor, yang, beginnings

Two = balance, union, receptive, yin

Three = communication, interaction, neutrality, birth, life, death

Four = creation, cardinal directions

Five = action, Pythagorean humanity

Six = reaction, responsibility, harmony

Seven = thought, consciousness, divine mystery

Eight = power, sacrifice, cosmic balance

Nine = completion, triple power of three

Ten = rebirth, divine power

The number twelve is especially symbolic as the number of universal fulfillment, manifesting its significance in countless examples, the twelve houses of the zodiac: Aries, Taurus, Gemini, Cancer, Leo, Virgo, Libra, Scorpio, Sagittarius, Capricorn, Aquarius, and Pisces.

Copernicus, the Polish mathematician and astronomer, created a map of his notion of the universe. The illustration depicts all the signs of the zodiac encircling his concept.

Reflected in the names of certain constellations, the labors of Heracles (Hercules) relate to the twelve houses. Glorious through Hera is the title conferred upon Heracles, as both god and mortal; Hera by inversion is Rhea. As the hero of the zodiac, Heracles was highly esteemed by the Heraclidae, who built a father image of him on the hills of Dorset in England (the giant at Cerne Abbas). Fascinating legends developed from the veneration of this Heracleopolitan hero. He was in service for twelve years to King Eurysheus who compelled him to perform the twelve labors.

Leo: The first labor for Heracles was to strangle the Lion of Nemea. For this task, he had 360 allies, which are the days of the zodiac. Nergal, the ruler of Leo, is the winged lion or sun of death. The Lion of Nemesis is another name for Ares, in Hebrew lion is *aria*. Glorying in his conquest of the lion, Heracles wore its skin as a trophy.

Scorpio: The second labor was the slaying of the nine-mortal-headed Hydra of Lerna. The hydra is the waters of Ti'amat representing the serpent of the zodiac, which in this instance had nine heads, and as soon as one head was lopped off, the monster grew another, making it an exceedingly difficult task.

Aries: The third labor was the capture of the live boar of Erymanthus.

Capricorn: The fourth Labor was outrunning the Arcadian Hind, sacred to Artemis, goddess of the wild.

The other labors followed, not necessarily in order of execution. Sagittarius: The shooting of the man-eating Stymphalian birds. Taurus: The Capture of the Cretan Bull. This bull was originally supposed to be a sacrifice to Poseidon, but somehow evaded this fate. Gemini: The Assassination of the king of Thrace. This was a most gruesome task because it entailed feeding the body of the king to the man-eating mares of Diomedes. Cancer: The killing of the ogre Geryon, and the stealth of his cattle. Virgo: The conquest of the Amazons. Heracles was commanded to fetch the girdle of their queen, Hippolyta. At some point, Heracles seduced fifty virgin daughters of Thespus; however, one managed to escape his advances.

Libra: The Quest for the Golden Apples of the Hesperides, the Daughters of the Night. Heracles slew the dragon Lagon who guarded the tree in the garden of the Hesperides. The garden lay where the sun still shone long after it had set over Greece. A sign for

Libra represents the setting sun. This was the land of Hyperborean, which was north of the Danube's source, and was the great center of the cult of Boreas, the north wind. The golden apples of Hera are the stars.

Aquarius: The diversion of the rivers to cleanse the Augean Stables. Augeas owned vast herds of cattle, obviously requiring considerable cleansing maintenance!

Pisces: Heracles descended to Hades to trap the three-headed hound Cerberus, for delivery to the king. For this, his last labor, Heracles attained immortality. It is interesting that some of the exploits of the Greek hero Theseus closely resemble those of Heracles.

Further examples demonstrate the extent of the implication of the number twelve: the twelve disciples of Jesus—Simon Peter, Andrew, James the son of Zebedee and his brother John, Philip, Bartholomew, Thomas, Matthew the publican, James the son of Alpheus, Lebbaeus, Simon the Canaanite, and Judas Iscariot. Some maintain that each disciple represents a house of the zodiac.

The pictorial arrangement of the twelve tribes of Israel around the tabernacle corresponds to the order of the zodiac. According to the *Yalkut Shimoni*, the standards of the twelve tribes correspond to the signs of the zodiac:

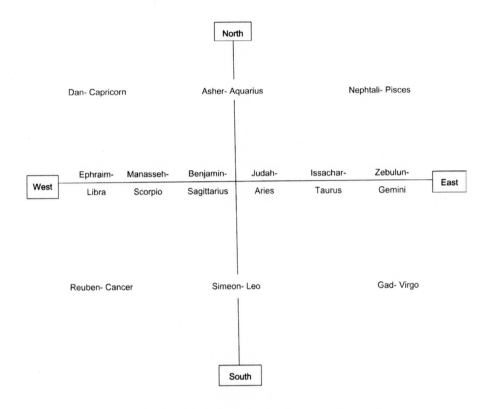

East: Judah/Aries, Issachar/Taurus, and Zebulon/Gemini

South: Reuben/Cancer, Simeon/Leo, and Gad/Virgo

West: Ephraim/Libra, Manasseh/Scorpio, and Benjamin/Sagittarius

North: Dan/Capricorn, Asher/Aquarius, and Naphtali/Pisces

The houses of the zodiac also correspond to the twelve tribes, each having its own ruler.

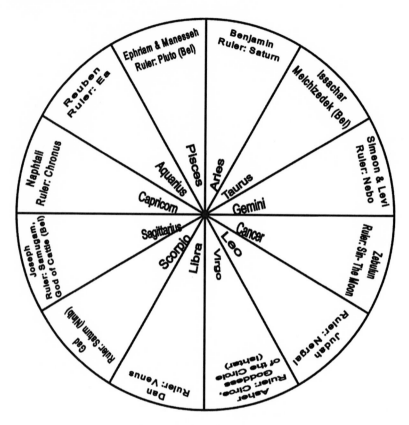

Benjamin: Aries/Saturn
Issachar: Taurus/Bel, known here as Melchizedek
Simeon and Levi: Gemini/Nebo
Zebulon: Cancer/the Moon
Judah: Leo/Nergal
Asher: Virgo/Circe, goddess of the circle; Dan: Libra/Ishtar/Venus:
Gad: Scorpio/Ninib/Saturn
Joseph: Sagittarius/Samugan, god of cattle; Naphtali: Capricorn /
Chronus; Reuben: Aquarius /Ea
Ephraim and Manasseh: Pisces/Bel, here known as Pluto.

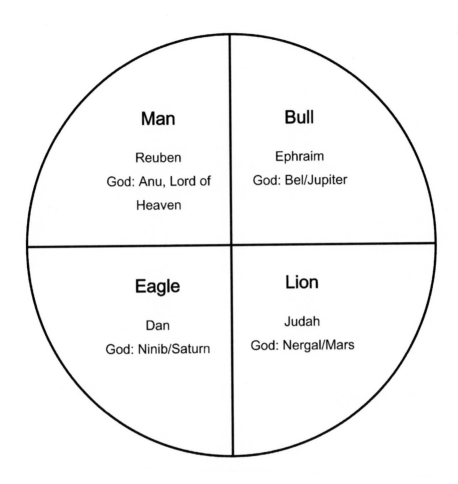

Both the Books of Ezekiel and Revelation are divided into four quarters, each ruled by the bull, the lion, the eagle, and the man. These correspond to the tribes of Israel: Ephraim the bull, Judah the lion, Dan the eagle, and Reuben the man. The Benjaminites gave Israel her first king: Saul. Some members of this tribe worshipped Belial, the prince of darkness (the opposite of Melchizedek). One of the clans of the tribe of Benjamin was Bela, followers of Bel, lord of the zodiac. This is confusing with two conflicting stem-names, because Bel was known as Jupiter,

Earth, Zedec, etc. Belial was his opposite as The Evil One, his followers being referred to as the Sons of Darkness. In the time of Joshua, many Israelites turned to the worship of Ba'al and Astoreth, and henceforth were considered outsiders.

The Dead Sea Scrolls reveal much about the Qumran Community. Relevant to this chapter -twelve men were the pillars of the community, and their juries were composed of twelve good men and true.

In the beginning, the twelve months of the year had Canaanite names, but later, some of the Babylonian names came into use:

January: *Tebeth*

February: *Shebat*

March: *Adar*

April: *Abib or Nisan*

May: *Ziv or Iyyar*

June: *Sivan*

July: *Tammuz*

August: *Ab*

September: *Elul*

October: *Ethanim or Tishri*

November: *Bul or Marchewan*

December: *Chislev*

The book of Revelation resonates with mystical numbers, the number twelve being the most prominent. Twelve precious stones formed the foundation for the New Jerusalem. Believing precious stones to have been gifts from the gods, every of the month of the zodiac has its own gem, bringing luck for the wearer, or possibly misfortune for others. "The first was jasper; the second, sapphire; the third, a chalcedony;

the fourth, an emerald; the fifth, sardonyx; the sixth, sardius; the seventh, chrysolite; the eighth, beryl; the ninth, a topaz; the tenth, a chrysoprase; the eleventh, a jacinth; the twelfth, an amethyst" (Revelation 21:19–20). Each of the tribes was sealed with twelve thousand; the New Jerusalem "had twelve gates, and at the gates twelve angels, and names written thereon, which are the names of the twelve tribes of the children of Israel" (Revelation 21:12). "And the wall of the city had twelve foundations, and in them the names of the twelve apostles of the Lamb" (Revelation 21:14). An image of the Virgin Mary shows her with a halo bearing twelve stars.

The number eight is sacred to many cultures worldwide because it is the number of cosmic balance. Venus has eight points; the cuttlefish, venerated in Crete and Magnesia (Asia Minor), has eight tentacles, and eight is the number of the sacred white horses of China.

The Babylonians revered the number seven because it is a complete number. The Gnostics divided the heavens into seven spheres and because there are seven seals to the fountain of life—Aquarius—one must travel through seven constellations to reach it. Celsus, a pagan philosopher, refers to the ancient mysteries, comparing the Christian ways of the soul to heaven with that of the ancient systems of seven heavens. The principle of seven steps is found in the design of Chartres Cathedral conveying the representation of the seven liberal arts, the study of which guided seekers of knowledge on their quest for the hidden light. Creation took seven days. There are seven days in a week. In the Jewish reckoning, Saturday is the seventh day because Saturn/ Resh/Zababa/Sabbath was the seventh planet. According to exaltations, the first day is allotted to the sun, and the second to the moon: sun's day; moon's day; Deis Martis/Martu—Tuesday; Wodan's day- Wednesday; Thor's day, Tor or Tau—Thursday; Fria's day/Venus—Friday; Saturn's day—Saturday. The rainbow is comprised of seven colors. The musical scale consists of seven notes. There were seven stages of initiation to the cult of Ishtar/Astarte, goddess of prostitution (one might conjecture what they were and the reasons for them). The Phoenicians created a divine group of seven *khabirim*, mighty ones who were sons of Sydyk the Just, Lord of All Seven. Seven planets are the seven keys, the seven lights of heaven, although the ancients knew of only five plus the sun and the moon. The seven, according to Ptolemy in the second century were these:

1. The sun/*shamash/utu*

2. Saturn in Libra

3. The moon

4. Jupiter/Cancer

5. Mars/Capricorn

6. Venus/Pisces

7. Mercury/Virgo.

The Pleiades is a configuration of seven stars in the constellation of Orion, which seems to figure prominently in the alignment of many earthly structures such as certain European cathedrals, as well as the pyramids. Supposedly, one may be enlightened to the mysteries of heaven by appreciating the values of the treasures of the earth, in other words the seven metals: Jupiter—tin, Luna—silver, Saturn—lead, Venus—copper, Mars—iron, Sol—gold, and Mercury—quicksilver.

Wisdom's house has seven pillars (Proverbs 9:1). Samson's hair was braided in seven locks (Judges 16:13). To atone for a broken vow, seven sacrifices were required (2 Samuel 21:6). Sabbath, rest or *reseph* is the seventh planet, Saturn, called Great God and Lord of Heaven. The number for the serpent of the zodiac is seven, representing the universe and eternity. Revelation refers to seven many times, the first of which is in chapter one, verse four referring to the seven churches in Asia: "The mystery of the seven stars which thou sawest in my right hand, and the seven golden candlesticks. The seven stars are the angels of the seven churches; and the seven candlesticks which thou sawest are the seven churches." St. John the Divine sees seven angels with seven trumpets, and seven candlesticks, seven stars, seven lamps, and "a book written and on the backside, sealed with seven seals," revealing that the seven seals must be broken to open the scroll. The last seven words spoken by Christ on the cross are especially revered.

The number four is the arithmetic symbol for anything in physical form. There are four winds, four cherubim of Kaballah: Taurus /ox/ earth, Leo/lion/fire, Scorpio/eagle for air and scorpion for earth, Aquarius/ water. Further examples of the implication of the number four are, for example: four gods governed the four regions of the ancient world, four cardinal points of the compass, four seasons, and four mysterious letters of Torah. In the book of Revelation, the four figures were the lion, the ox, the man, and the eagle, similar to the four cherubim of Kaballah and the zodiac.

From the very earliest times, the number three has been hugely significant because it represented the triple *tau*: the temple of Jerusalem, the Holy of Holies, and the temple of Yahweh. For many, it is sublime as the holy Trinity of the Christian godhead: the Father, the Son, and the Holy Ghost. In Masonry, the number three holds sway and is of great importance, chiefly the three principle tenets of Freemasonry referring to the three foremost columns: the master pillar, the journeyman pillar, and the apprentice pillar. They also refer to the three grand masters and the three virtues of faith, hope and charity.

Throughout the history of humankind, the use of numbers establishes the patterns and order of nature, reflecting our expression of cosmic and natural wonders.

Warriors and Wanderers

Strange megaliths, circles of stones, and other curious landmarks dot landscapes worldwide, inviting investigation as to their meaning, the interpretations for which are ongoing projects. The wandering tribes of the ancient world who were responsible for these remarkable markers built them as lasting memorials to their gods, influencing the indigenous peoples with their own religion. Reflecting upon the message of these stone edifices, they direct our thinking to the zodiacal imprint.

The Cro-Magnons were the world's first mariners, and by applying a great knowledge of astronomy, were able to ply their trade everywhere. The Amurru considered themselves as "their children." The wanderers, whether by choice or conquest, always alluded to themselves as the children of their particular god, by which others recognized them.

However, three peoples figure prominently as the foremost traders and wanderers of ancient times. They are referred to in the Bible as the Amurru (Amorites) who were the mariners, the Kassites (Shasu) who were the traders, and the Hurri, the artisans. These three tribes combined to form an invincible force, and as the roots of civilization, they are the most important group in this story. Known as the Sons of Anak, the Anakim, they became the Dioscuri and Hellenes, the Princes of Siut and the Princes of the Serpent Mountain; whose symbol the serpent represents the circle of the zodiac. Interestingly, to describe the world in which they lived, the Amorites drew a circle and placed upon it their part of the world. Conceivably, it served as their representation of the cycle of nature and the cosmic order of the universe. This formidable alliance ruled in Mesopotamia, Egypt, and the islands of the Persian Gulf. They had a great deal in common: metals, astrology, astronomy, and trading. These giants of the Bible merited other titles: the Children of Eden and Children of the Third Son. The Koran refers to Adam as a race: Cain, Abel, Seth, being the Amurru, the Hurri, and the Kassites. The Surena of the Kassites were the most noble of all the tribes, entitled with the long-standing right of crowning kings. Wherever the megalithic trails lead, there we will find these Sons of Anak. Eventually, they were known variously as the Three Tribes of Sparta, the Three Tribes of Mycenae, and the Three Tribes of the Etruscans.

From as early as 4000 BC, the Amurru traded in Britain and Denmark, where they lodged in summer camps for the collection of amber, trading their pearls and shells from the Persian Gulf. Together with the Hurri, they were the Heracleopolitan Dynasties IX and X. Some Hurrians were Hittite kings. Although they worshipped many gods, their foremost deities were Teshub the weather god and Hepa the sun goddess. Heracles was the father god of the Hurrians, and Hebe of Egypt their mother goddess. They were inspired with the thought that upon his death, their king became a god. When the Heraclidae arrived in Britain, they brought their zodiacal religion with them, for which they built a lasting memorial—Stonehenge—that also served as their center for trade and learning. By reputation, giants populated the west country of Britain, probably the Amurru. The Hurrians, the priestly tribe who conducted the religious ceremonies, were mound builders. This is an important fact because only the Heraclidae, as the Children of the Zodiac were entitled to royal burial, signified by a double ring of stones under a gigantic mound. Mounds signify the Earth Mother.

Vanquished around 2040 BC, the Heraclidae, from their rallying point in the Caucasus, became the builders of Minoan Crete, assuming the name of Dioscuri, the twins—Gemini. The priests were the Dryads/Druids.

By 1800 BC, trade flourished everywhere. As tribes fell from power in one place, they scattered and regrouped in other strategic vantage points, maintaining a tight hold on all the trade routes by land, rivers and the sea, the zodiacal religion spread and maintained wherever they went. The last home of the Heraclids was Anu/Urartu.

Standing at the estuaries of the Adonis and Phaedrus rivers, Byblos in Phoenicia served the Amurru as their port. Around 3000 BC, the first keel ships were built here, being the prototype for all that followed. A fleet patrolled the waters between Byblos and Crete plying trade. Perfect for these seagoing vessels, the tall cedars of Lebanon were immensely useful, providing wood for the axes with which to fell them. The Egyptians used the oil extracted from the trees for embalming.

Bethel, the headquarters of the priesthood, supported the priestly college. It was here that the largest megalithic temple of Baal/Bel existed. Mari, the center of administration for the Amurru, destroyed by Khammurabi in 1531 BC, is known now as Tel el Hariri, House of the God Ares. As the Dioscuri, they ruled Egypt. Sinai was the most ancient place of their habitation from where, in a circle, they controlled and tracked the whole of the ancient world. They created the first alphabet in the Luwain language. According to the sacred calendar, they were of the house of Heth, which at Sinai was the house of Cancer. Eventually these tribes evolved into the Germanic race.

The Sumerians arrived from Dilmun around 4000 BC, but this begs the question of who preceded them in Dilmun? Dilmun was thought to be the home of the Annunaki, the pantheon of gods headed by Anu. Possibly, the Annunaki were the ancestors of the Sumerians, who invented the wheel and the pillar, both of which are crucial links in the history of the zodiac. Over one thousand small, pictographic clay tablets were discovered in Erech, (the sacred city of Anu,) and the literally tens of thousands of clay tablets give us a vivid description of the life and times of the Sumerians. Described in epic poems, we can easily discern their philosophy and religious conviction, and recognize the gods and goddesses of the zodiac. Perhaps even earlier are the Laws of Eshnunna, written in Akkadian. The Sumerians patronized Bau/Subat, goddess of Aquarius, and attributed their skills in medicine to the gods. The rules of agriculture were credited to the god Ninurta, who is Saturn/Scorpio. Due to a Sumerian recipe for beer that recently has been unearthed, we can give them credit for giving humankind its first booze. Taken from a four thousand-year-old cuneiform tablet, modern brewers have recreated this recipe calling it Ninkasi, commemorating the Kassite goddess of beer, proving that these ancients certainly knew a thing or two!

After the Hyksos fell from power in Egypt, the Hittites continued to dwell in the surrounding lands in Libya, having strongholds in Palestine and Syria.

The Hittites, who flourished from 1700 to 1200 BC, were the sons of Heth, a son of Canaan. The name Hittite stems from this, so the mythology of Mesopotamia, and therefore the zodiac, influenced not only their lives but also the Hurrians with whom they are closely linked. Migrants from the Hittite empire took their newly developed iron-working skills across southern Europe as well as their religious convictions. The Hittites were using hieroglyphic writing for the Hurrian pantheon of gods by the thirteenth century before Christ. In the museums worldwide, there are more than five hundred thousand cuneiform tablets in existence, holding literary and scientific information dating from the Sumerian period.

Charging across the deserts in their chariots, the Hyksos invaded Egypt around 2000 BC, conquering the pharaohs. The chariot was not only a new mode of transportation but also a highly efficient vehicle for war, striking terror in the locals. The name Hyksos means rulers of foreign lands, but when these princes of the Khassa nation poured down from the Kahsiari Mountains into Egypt, half of them took their power in Babylonia as the Kassites. Arriving with horses, which always hereafter were associated with them, they supplied the sacred white horses to Persia from whom the Arabian horses of today are descended. When a Hyksos warrior died, his horse and his sacred axe (*Sagitta*) were buried with him because they were held in such high esteem. Now here is the tie to the zodiacal house of Sagittarius: their light cavalry, the Sagittari, were famous throughout ancient history as the mounted bowmen, becoming the Children of Sagittarius.

These desert/shepherd kings not only introduced the chariot to Egypt, but also their zodiacal religion. A mixed group of Asiatic people together with the Khabiri evolved into the twelve tribes of Israel. The

65

nickname for the Khabiri was the Wanderers, because as nomadic people they could not be relegated to one god or planet. Khab are stars in the map of heaven and the related earth.

The kings of the castle were the Kassites/Kadachi, referring to the massive fortresses with which they protected themselves. They were the lords of the north wind, Buriash. At no other time in the history of Palestine do we find so many strongly fortified settlements that are more reminiscent of castles than of towns. These wild people were robber tribes, living in the mountain valleys at the gorge of the river Zab. They sported horsehair crests on fringed turbans and hunted with long bows and lassos. Notorious for cracking their enemies over the head with their axes, they deserved their reputation of being fearsome warriors. In Egypt, the Kassites raised colossal statues, commandeered by Rameses. The land of Lullabi—the house of the double eagle, Scorpio—was their homeland, which stretched from Baghdad through Kermanshah to Hamadan and Teheran. Both Sargon and his grandson Naram Sin waged war with them because they controlled the trade routes supplying Babylonia. The Kassites ruled Babylonia until about 1140 BC. The names Kassi, Kossain, and Cossack all refer to descendants of these magnificent people, who even today remain connected with banking, cash, and arms. The goddess of the Kassites was Cassiopeia who represented tin and metals. Renowned beer drinkers, they probably used that recipe from the Sumerians.

The importance of these tribes to this story is that their royal tribe of inherited nobility, the Surena, not only is connected to the Sagittari, but also is supposedly linked to Caspar of the famous Magi, and as extensive traders, they spread their religion wherever they went.

We have established that the conqueror Sargon was crucial to the origins of the zodiac. He had an extraordinary history. His mother was a temple priestess, who, for some reason best known to her, put her baby into a tar basket and launched it upon the river (reminiscent of the story of Moses). Aqqi (Aquarius), a gardener, rescued Sargon and reared him. Sargon's seal bears the sign of Aquarius. He rose to great heights, becoming the world's first emperor, by creating the first powerful Semitic empire, with his domains spreading from Elam to the

Mediterranean Mesopotamia. As mentioned earlier, maintaining his power required precise information to find raw materials so essential for his enterprises. Sargon made the first serious attempt to map the world relating to the heavens, because he realized the absolute necessity for knowledge of the many tribes, their lands, and above all, their gods. He collected astronomical observations for one of his libraries. Additionally, one of the first great libraries of astrological writing was created in Sargon's time. Much later, Callisthenes, the Greek historian, went to Babylon with Alexander the Great (356–323 BC) where he discovered a series of astronomical observations dating back nineteen hundred years.

Sargon acted upon informed and well-advised sources. The earliest signs of the decani (Decan means thirty degrees of a sign of the zodiac. Ref: *Compact Edition of the Oxford English Dictionary—1971*) possibly came from the Pyramid Texts (2700 BC), which tells of "one god— wholly present in entire circle." Extensive research, charting, and arranging of heaven and earth was carried out, and he compiled this knowledge into geographical locations. He is reputed to have traveled to all the places he included in his map, ensuring that commerce thrived. His charting of the zodiac was one of the greatest, most influential enterprises from which humankind benefits even today. Under his rule, the Semitic Akkadian language prevailed, and Sargon was addressed (among many other titles) as the God of Agade. This great king claimed Ishtar as his lover and protector. She bestowed upon him the title of Sharru-Kin, Righteous Ruler. He proclaimed himself as Overseer of Ishtar, Anointed Priest of Anu, and Great Righteous Priest of Enlil. An extremely pious man, who, when building his palace, inscribed the gates with the names of the gods to demonstrate his devotion to them.

The grandson of Sargon, Naram Sin, upon becoming king of Akkad, continued with the great work of charting the zodiac. To establish the map he required a treaty, binding together the nations of Egypt and Elam. The fact that Naram Sin fought a coalition of seventeen kings, suggests that this could have been when fixed boundaries established the earthly houses of the gods in accordance with the zodiac. The Khiti Treaty was drawn up mentioning all the gods of each house, "twelve good men and true," with Ninib acting as judge. Undoubtedly, this caused considerable concern, as the dynasty of Akkad could now locate most of its requirements with a very precise map. All the surrounding lands became the provinces of the gods, and it would fare very ill for any of the inhabitants who failed to subscribe to their well-being.

The highly valued and revered religious document of the Phoenicians is *The Emerald Tablet,* whose author was Hermes Trismegistus. Its ancient wisdom inspired the Abrahamic religions: Judaism, Christianity, and Islam. Alchemists throughout the ages referred to the secret formula within it.

The Phoenicians were the sea peoples in the Levant who lived around 1500 BC. Great fishing tycoons and superb mariners, they controlled trade. They originated in the Persian Gulf (Dilmun) and were part of the Chaldean nation whose origin stems from the Amurru. Originally as Canaanites, they spoke one of the Semitic groups of languages, using a phonetic alphabet. The Phoenicians form the connection with the tribes of the zodiacal religion, because they inherited the secret knowledge of the zodiacal mapping of the heavens and earth. Understandably, they endeavored to keep it to themselves, but to no avail. Invaluable to shipping and commerce, it was a formidable source of information. The whole pattern of their lives revolved around the zodiac. They placed all of history in the heavens using signs and symbols. The Phoenicians created a divine group of seven *khabirim*, Mighty Ones, who were Sons of Sydyk the Just, the Lord of all Seven. They added an eighth *khabir*, Eshmun, who was exalted and greater than the rest. From Mesopotamia, the Hebrews brought their own hallowed stories, handed down by word of mouth, many of which had their origins in Akkadian and Canaanite literature. The *Texts of Ugarit* also were a source of these legends that had originated in the Canaanite culture.

The Chaldeans were the Amurru and the Kassites who formed a nation in the islands of the Persian Gulf. Establishing themselves in the south land of Babylonia, in the Caucasus and Palestine, they were of the house of Dis-Kaldis, worshiping Bel. When in power, they reorganized the zodiac, and in 747 BC, forced Assyria to bring Nebo up from his house of Virgo placing him in Aquarius to represent Man in the three houses: Aquarius, Pisces, and Capricorn. After the decline of their empire, the Chaldeans wandered the world as magicians, and astrologers, spreading the cult of the zodiac, for which they were famous, throughout the Egyptian, Greek and Roman worlds. The Chaldeans inhabited three strips of land in the Thracian Sea. They were not so blind when they chose this spot to settle, because here was the home of the gods, the land of mist and mystery. This was the land of the god Hades, who was famous for his helmet, which, supposedly conferring invisibility upon the wearer was in great demand among the gods. A three-headed dog, Cerberus, guarded the shades of Hades wherein the dead were received. The Cyclops, those horrific giants with the circling eyes, carefully guarded the entrance and whoever managed to get through (such as the ever-curious Greeks) usually did not return. This notoriety justified its name of the Land of the Dead.

Placed second in the biblical table of nations, the Assyrians are the Children of Shem. Akin to the Hebrews in type and language, and in their approach to religion, they retained all the old Babylonian gods. Asshur, divine king of the military state, was above them all, the earthly king being his representative. The Assyrians believed themselves to be under the divine protection of Asshur, and like countless other warriors, presented their plans of diplomacy and military strategy before the sun god for his approbation. There are many elaborate rituals and prayers attesting to their belief in oracles. The inscription of Tiglath-Pileser, an Assyrian king, bears testimony. "Asshur, the great lord, who rules the host of gods, who endows with scepter and crown, establishes royalty; Bel, the lord, the king of all the Annunaki, father of the gods, lord of countries; Sin the wise, lord of the crown, the exalted in luminous brilliancy; Shamash, the judge of heaven and earth, who sees the evil deeds of the enemy; Raman the Mighty, who floods the countries of the enemies, their lands, their houses; Ninib the Strong, who destroys evil-doers and enemies and lets men find their heart's desire; Ishtar, the firstborn of the gods, who makes battles fierce; ye great gods, who the governors of heaven and earth whose onslaught is battle and destruction, who have exalted the royalty of Tiglath-Pileser the great one, the believed of our hearts."

Quite often, Asshur's emblem appears as a human figure. Ending with an appendage like the tail of a bird, it could be a dove, the emblem of Ishtar. A wheel, like the circle of the zodiac, is behind the figure enclosing an inner circle, or sun disk, from which stem four rays. Above, it bears the horns of Bel, and below, the lightning forks of Adad. The four rays possibly represent the four realms. The character of the god sometimes depends upon the scene in which the king is active: if it is a battle then Asshur hovers above the king in a protective attitude, carrying a bow. The arrow imparts a message to all impressing them of his power and protection that the king enjoys. If it is a peaceful ceremony, then the bow is lower, with the right hand raised in an attitude of blessing. The gods they worshipped reflected the traits of the Assyrians: Adad, the god of the storm, and Ishtar, mistress of the soldier home from the war, and goddess of love and lust. The Assyrians, although warlike, cruel and ambitious, were devoted to history. This was not a commercial people; they appreciated art, but usually left the execution of it to others. However, if the Assyrians were the early Akkadians, their early art was very fine. The seals of Sargon show a great understanding of intricate portrayal. Their king was warrior and defender of his people, and the kings of Assyria regarded themselves as Sons of Ninib, because he was their favorite god, and they benefited from his divine influence. When Anu retreated to the sky itself, Ninib assumed his role of ruler of the house of Capricorn. In Capricorn, the god is at his peak, or exaltation. Ninib is Chronus or Saturn, so historically all the Assyrians were his sons. Ashbanipal, the king of Assyria in 668 BC, a learned scholar and mathematician, maintained he received the gift of writing from the gods. He acquired an enormous number of clay tablets to form his extensive libraries, one of which contained over twenty-two thousand books for which borrowers had to take a number. The libraries were available solely to the priests and scribes, making them enormously powerful, and keeping control firmly in their grasp. They impelled even the kings to accept their word as law, thus accomplishing everything in the name of religion: the zodiac. As they wandered, by maintaining their methods and rites of worship, they kept their traditions in place, influencing the various indigenous peoples with whom they came into contact. They firmly established themselves, and their religion, into their new locales.

The Sons of Dis were the Chaldeans of north and south Mesopotamia, and three hundred of the nobility fought each other to the death, rather than flee from the Scythians. In Gaul, they were the Children of Dis, or Sol-de-Uri, from which the word soldier is derived. Around 1000 BC, these Sons of Dis arrived in Sumer from the islands of the Persian Gulf, establishing their kingdoms in Urartu in the north, and what became known as Chaldea, in the south. The Urartians carried round shields depicting figures of zodiacal signs and gods that they considered as somewhat sacred. From these people stem many myths and legends, and finally they appear in Rome as the first twins, Romulus and Remus.

The Gauls conferred upon themselves the sobriquet "Children of Dis," Dis/Anu. Kaldis is the same as Celts; kal is house or place. Legend has it that Anu created these sons of the house of Dis. Moved by pity of the suffering of humankind, wrought by the cruelty of both the raging sun Shamash, and the destruction by plague and disease by Nergal the lord of death, Anu decided to create a new nation, formulated by his sons. Thus, it came about that the three chosen nations merged to become Chaldea or Kaldis, in the islands, later known as the Persian Gulf. The Sons of Anu were, according to Assyrian inscriptions, Martu. The conquering hordes reveled in their victories over these Children. Most famous was Sennacherib who boasted of his dispersal of the Children of Eden, thereby increasing his power. This truly significant achievement immensely added to his luster, because of the reputation of the Babylonians. Held in high esteem as former Heraclids, and especially favored by the gods, they had been feared as being invincible.

The Sons of Zadok, *Rex Deus*—kings of god—was the title of the Merovingian kings who originally came from Scythia, appearing around AD 400. They claim a bloodline from Jesus of Nazareth. The Merovingians, who revered Solomon, are closely connected with the Knights Templar absorbing their knowledge of the ancient mysteries. Originally known as the Sorcerer Kings, dragons and sea serpents are associated with them.

The people of the zodiac who lived in the four regions: houses of the

71

zodiac, were children of their own particular god, and as such, merited the honor of burial beneath a double ring of stones. The stones represent the zodiac, thus marking them as royal children of the zodiac.

Like us, they lived.

So, What Was the Zodiac?

Was the zodiac a gift from the gods? Credit has been given to a number of the primary Babylonian deities for their participation in its creation, but mere mortals put it to use. It has certainly played a key role in our history, keenly influencing many lives across the centuries.

In the beginning, it was a very precise chart of the heavens and earth—"as in heaven so below." The necessity for order promoted the concept of allotting areas for the gods to rule. The mansions of the gods described the exact location and boundaries of the rulers of these realms, so that due worship and obedience was accredited to them in their appropriate houses. This was to not only ensure peace and security for themselves, but also to prevent the constant warring between the deities eager for power. It was hoped that the ability of the priest-kings to read the signs successfully would result in prosperity and peace. The changing seasons invoked the prescribed ritual and devotion to the deities, and the gods were ascribed credit for the invention of all aspects of daily life: the plough, pickaxe, canals for irrigation, and everything else needed for progress, sustenance, and general well-being.

The various gods worshipped by the pagans were reflections of the many-faceted One God, "He Who is Without a Second," the great god Anu. Anu was the sky that was divided into twelve portions, becoming the zodiac with its twelve houses or constellations. The belief is that the order in which the twelve zodiacal signs were placed reveals the sequence of the different stages of creation. Some acquaint God as the sun, and the twelve signs as the twelve apostles. And if Christ is associated with Aquarius, he would be an unmistakable link with Nebo.

Reaching back into prehistory, legends and myths relate similar events of the most ancient peoples, making convincing argument that the same gods are peculiar to many cultures. This is due to the rituals of worship being intertwined, following the prescribed devotions and oracles of the priest-kings. The greater parts of the zodiacal signs were discovered in Sumer and Elam. Some passages in the texts of the Nag Hammadi Library reveal that seven planets were known, and more significantly, the twelve signs of the zodiac were portrayed. These writings are over two thousand years old and are a substantial source of the Gnosticism schools of thought. They shed light on early wisdom and subsequent beliefs and rituals of those seeking immortal and divine knowledge. Religion was fundamental, a bond of unity, and ground of political rights, authority and progress.

The story of the zodiac is a history of the earth according to the beliefs of the compilers of the charts, and the relationship between heaven and earth. The historians created the story by stating the facts as had been related to them from the early inhabitants. They concurred that a very ancient race had existed, although having always been present none knew their origins. Most people could claim they came from different points of the compass, but not these people: the earth was their inheritance from time immemorial. The race of formidable giants, were capable of moving tremendous blocks of stone, and known by the Egyptians as Aduma, Adam. The Hebrews knew them as Edom, a name of Esau, and through him, a race of people, the Edomites. According to the Hebrews, the kings of Edom were symbolic of a world formless and void, thus ruling before the formation of the zodiac. These were the first men, whose racial or tribal name was Amurru or Amorite. Other people could claim an earthly father or founder of their tribe, but not the Amorites—they had no founding father but God. They were his first creation, and it was from the Amurru that Sargon acquired the fabled star tables. The question remains, however, of how the Amurru came into their possession. We do know that the zodiac was created from the

74

sacred calendar. The first signs of a written alphabet were found at Sinai, and the first star tables were discovered in Kish on the sarcophagi of the Amorite Princes of Siut as early as 3600 BC, inferring that the Amurru were the first people to have a religion using what would become the zodiacal signs as we now know them. However, the zodiac is quite possibly over eight thousand years old, and if we consider the Turkish temple dating back twelve thousand years, with the circles and depiction of animals, the format of a prototype of the zodiac cannot be dismissed. Indeed, there are some who believe the origins go back as far as fourteen thousand years. The Amurru were the first holy men, or priests, of the zodiac. Maps of the thirty-six Egyptian decans were copied from the coffin lids of the Heraclidean dynasties. They are the oldest known decani lists, which are the originals of the modern zodiac created around 2732 BC.

These sufficiently informed people understood the precession of the equinoxes well enough to calculate the formulae, which inspired them. The earliest astrology possibly may be traced to India, with the word zodiac stemming from the Sanskrit word *sodi*, denoting a path. The earliest markings of the seasons appear around 5000 BC, and the earliest temples previously thought to have dated from six thousand, five hundred years ago. The construction of the Sphinx may well have been the first indicator by which to embark on such an enterprise because of its precise location in relation with the stars and the houses of Leo and Aquarius.

There are many traditions concerning the inception of the zodiac, among them that it was actually the god Ea who invented the circle; the Egyptian god Thoth is given credit for the celestial hierarchy; and Bel with the first charting of the heavens and earth.

The zodiac is an imaginary belt in the celestial sphere on either side of the apparent path of the sun among the stars. Its width originally was determined to include the orbits of the sun, moon, and the planets Venus, Mars, Jupiter, and Saturn. This belt was referred to as the Girdle of Ishtar, as the moon goddess; the zodiacal constellations were called the houses of the moon. Due to the precession, or westward motion, of the equinoxes along the ecliptic, the sun's apparent journey, the starting points of the four seasons arrive earlier each year, altering the alignment of the stars. The sun begins its journey around the zodiac in Pisces and continues in a seemingly retrograde movement. Taking seventy-two years to move one degree of a precessional cycle, it takes the earth 25,920 years to make a complete precessional cycle, with the sun spending 2,160 years in each house. The eleventh millennium marked the Age of Leo; the age of Aries began around 2000 BC; the Age of Pisces, which is ending, started about 140 BC, and the Age of Aquarius is now dawning.

Initially there were twelve divinities, the twelve constellations combined into a zodiac with thirteen houses in all, to include the house for Shamash. The Greeks later modified this to the twelve houses we know today. The sun and the moon are the explainers of destiny, and the seven planets decided the fate of humankind. Each of these great planets was designated its own house on earth in which to live, with a deity as its ruler.

Stelae are pictorial calendars of the zodiacal or sacred year, and they are the tablets of destiny for the twelve constellations. The actual map of the zodiac was a considerable strategic undertaking. Silver plating had been invented, and bronze had already made an appearance, which explains Sargon's need to break the stranglehold on trade held by the Amurru, making his acquisition of the charts essential. His map was continued by his grandson Naram-Sin.

The suppositions of the correlation of heaven and earth were not limited to Mesopotamia. A quotation from the *Popul Vuh* of South America seems to indicate their awareness of the basis for the zodiacal formulae, "Four corners, four points of the arch of the sky, the round face of the earth," and perhaps the Mayan calendar, an early map of the world, was one of the earliest zodiacs. In Mesoamerican cultures there were four gods who created fire, and the calendar. Twelve more heavens were occupied by the gods of fire, earth, and sky. Planets exert an enormous influence on earth, and certainly, the ancients of both East and West were aware of this due to the natural rhythm of cycles. So through mathematical formulae, they were able to calculate the movement of the stars to make adjustments for their daily life and rituals.

The chart of the zodiac was made in relation to the calendar both sacred and civil, and the placing of the constellations over the land at a certain time of year pertained to the fixed zodiac. All information derived from the stars above related to the earth below and was put into calendrical, alphabetical and astrological order. To calculate the start of the new cycle of the zodiac they began at sunrise of the first day of the spring equinox, the house of Aries. They made the first chart when the sun was one degree in Virgo, which will appear in Pisces, the opposite sign, ready for the coming months of spring and summer.

It was determined that the ruler of the following constellation must be the son of the goddess of the previous one. These restrictions perpetuated the original concept of organizing the cycle of the year to establish order in the entire cosmos and upon earth. It was an explicit method of assigning the gods to their appropriate season, and allocating earthly houses for them to rule. For their well-being, the people were dependent upon the ruler of their house. Their belief was that the god bore responsibility for ensuring the order of the natural world and the cosmos, fertility of crops, and overall prosperity. This committed the populace to rendering due veneration and obedience.

Life in the barren hills of ancient Mesopotamia was a proving ground for religious ways. The belief in numerous deities and the powerful influence they wielded sprang from pre-historical sources. It seems entirely plausible that the so-called weird vagaries of these worshippers stemmed from the divine properties of both magic and mathematical formulae. The zodiac recorded for all time both the mysteries of faith and history.

The many peoples whose lives are associated with the pagan religion assimilated the legacy of the early civilizations preceding Sumer. This legacy was promoted by the creation of the zodiac as we know it today. It was first formed in Sumer, in the fertile valley that lies between the Tigris and the Euphrates, and although the original charting of the heavens is attributed to the Sumerians, they lived side by side with the original dwellers, the Amurru, Khassa, and the Hurrians. Astrology and astronomy of the Babylonians and Chaldeans frequently is referred to as Semitic, but the Amurru and the Hurrians have been found to be non-

Semitic. Following the practices of the old Pagan religion, they held the belief that the gods revealed their knowledge to them. Names were assigned to all things which had their own particular place in the universe.

In the Age of Taurus, the Sumerians began their calendar of worship, evolving into a firmly established religion, science, and language that was spread far afield by the wandering tribes on their migratory routes. Clay tablets found at Nippur reveal many astronomical terms. Nippur, which they called Nibiru, was Sumer's religious center, where the calendar of the relationship between the sun, moon and stars was created around 3800 BC. Niburu was one of the seven outer planets, known by the Sumerians as the Planet of the Crossings whose symbol was the cross, and thought to be the home of Anu when he deserted his earthly house. Sumerians enlightened us as to their beliefs in the origin of creation, humankind, and kingship by leaving records in thousands of clay tablets outlining precise details of their daily life and rituals. Their acknowledgment of the significance of the role of the stars moving across the heavens, conceptualized the formation of the gods and their Houses, and the cycle of life, was expanded by the Babylonians who were nothing if not organized. It was they who discovered Saros, the great cycle of years, after which the eclipses returned to their starting point, charting the passage of time through eternity.

The Babylonians, by using a single wedge, and employing the number sixty for their numerical reckoning, charted the stars to within a sixtieth of an hour. To reflect their importance in the heavenly hierarchy, the gods were assigned a number. However, the continual warring between them created friction, causing the division of land into areas of earthly kingship, to firmly establish their boundaries of jurisdiction and influence.

The ancient dwellers of the earth, and in particular, the Babylonians, believed that Zi inhabited the world, Zi meaning spirit. The divine beings known variously as Zi-Ana, the spirit of heaven; Zi-Ka, lord of the demons who was the spirit of the earth; Enlil, the lord of the winds, and Enki, lord of the earth. The observance of the daily changes that provided light and energy gave rise to the belief in these spirits. The fire, or rays of the sun as part of the sun, also came out of the mountains promoting the concept that the spirit of the sun dwelt in them. Whenever possible, they selected a mountain for each god and named it for him. The spirits, called Strong Ones, were the heavenly powers of sun, moon, stars, and all the forces of nature, with one Great Spirit, the divine force, over all. These Strong Ones, both good and evil, determined the condition and destiny of humankind. The principle of that life force which warms and animates the human body was believed to be of the same essence of the fires of heaven and thus imbued with the gifts of the divine master spirit, God. God rules by a fixed law and is perfect, a light shining in the darkness transmitting true knowledge. The magic fluid Sa carried life, health, and vigor that the gods could transmit to humankind. The soul received Sa at birth and at that moment the stars determined the soul's fate on earth. Referred to by the early Sumerians as the blood of Ea, Sa came from a mystical pond that never emptied, somewhere in the north to whence the gods returned for renewal.

When humans overcame their fear of the gods, they recognized the deities as superior beings, visualized in human form. As gods, they received gifts, worship and reverence of the community, and were highly influential in the daily comings and goings of the mortals. Their universe was a region where humans and gods existed, each in their allotted compartments. The earth, conceived as an inverted bowl or mountain, had its edges resting on the great watery deep. Humankind dwelt on the outer surface, and within its crust was the dark abode of the dead. Above and surrounding all was another hemisphere, the heaven, on the underside of which moved the sun, moon, and stars. The gods dwelt beyond this in a place of eternal light.

When the sun passed through the heavenly gates from east to west on its journey around the dome, the gods met at the eastern gate of the sunrise, over the Caspian Sea, to determine the fate of humankind and the destiny of the universe. To know the will of the gods, the priests studied the stars and the movements of the sun and the moon. The sun, without whose power the earth would perish, was Shamash or Babbar, and the moon was Sin or Nannar. Every city venerated many gods but also paid homage to its own particular deity. As an earthly area produced a new dynasty, the god whose realm it was, wielded supreme power. In addition to these regions ruled by the gods were the father and motherlands. Great temples were built for the most holy of gods, the heavenly deities. Ea's temple at Eridu was in Aquarius; Sin, the moon god's temple was at Ur in Cancer; the temple for Shamash was at Larsam, which naturally was in Leo; and Uruk in Libra was dedicated to Ishtar. Geographically laid out, the zodiac determined the exact location of the sphere of influence of the ruling deity. The Caucasus Mountains were the abode of the gods, the high place where the earth touched the sky, and where the blue mountains stood like sentinels surrounding Ararat, Ur-ar-tu, the solitary white mountain, their summit of the earth. The sky or Scythia, the land of the gods lay beyond. In the language of Akkad, the twin peaks of Ararat mean *mashu*, the twins. At dawn, the Scorpion Men who guarded the gates to Mashu released Shamash for him to make his daily journey across the sky. Here was the holy place on which the ark of Noah rested after the great flood.

All the forces of nature impressed the Babylonian. They were above him: supreme powers that he served and obeyed in humility and dependence, addressing him as lord. Yet mighty as the gods were, and exalted as they were above humanity, the Babylonians were profoundly conscious of the influence brought to bear by the divine world upon humankind. From the period when they felt themselves surrounded by manifold spirits of the natural world, to the time when they sought to do the will of the heavenly powers, they were ever the center of the play of forces of the other world.

The stars moving across the sky and the regularity of their movement spoke to them of the will of the gods and emitted divine influences. The winds, storms, earthquakes, eclipses, and actions of animals and the flight of birds all conveyed divine messages to those who could interpret them. Hence arose the immense mass of magical texts, the science of astrology, and the doctrine of omens.

The early watchers, when the zodiac was described, observed that the constellations appeared in different parts of the arc of heaven after they had disappeared into the underworld. For example, Virgo would reappear in the constellation of Pisces and vice versa, giving rise to the myth of Persephone and Hades. So as the constellations appeared, they were conceived as demons rising from the underworld. When one constellation appeared in another's space, the symbol for this period would be a composite of both. For instance, Nisrock, the eagle, represented both Scorpio and Libra, which when first combined, boasted the symbol of the claws of the eagle. The claws later became the scales of justice and balance for Libra. Scorpio adopted the scorpion as its symbol.

Approach to a greater god was made only through a priest, so consequently the priests wielded enormous power and were truly priest-kings. The main college for the priesthood was at Bethel.

As the priests gradually assumed kingship they became the representative of the gods, and as such, were holy. Eventually when the king's duties became too onerous, lesser priests carried out the affairs of the temples. These lower ranking priests became the astrologers, seers and scribes, and the first officials of government.

By 2700 BC, the ancient world portioned into four realms, represented the four cardinal points. Subsequently, it was divided into twelve regions. The four regions represented the four known planets and the four cherubim of Kabbalah: earth/Taurus, sun/Leo, air/Scorpio, and water/Aquarius. The first realm was Bel's: Aries, Taurus, and Gemini. Leo/Shamash ruled Nergal's realm, comprising Cancer, Leo, and Virgo. Ninib/ Saturn ruled over the third region: Libra, Scorpio, and Sagittarius. Anu ruled the fourth region: Capricorn, Aquarius, and Pisces. All souls gathered here for judgment before being escorted by the Ferryman Nibiru/Nebo to the next house for another zodiacal year. Merodach (the Sumerian name for god) instituted the year, dividing it into twelve months; every month divided into three decans, the rulers of which exercised their authority for a period of ten days. This was under the direction of Nibiru.

The mountains were the homes of the gods, relating to their place in heaven. Boundary stones were set up, and the first one was in Bit-Adini or Beth Eden, now called Adana in north Syria. This is the house of Adanu, the First Man.

The *Enuma Elish,* the book of the gods of heaven and earth, was a codified astrological series, a section of which was contained in a clay tablet with cuneiform signs pressed into wax. Thousands of clay tablets, discovered in Iraq in the nineteenth century, describe the furious battles of the gods fighting for power and territory, struggling for supremacy and control.

The zodiac was formed by dividing the circle into twelve (thirteen at the outset) each with a celestial house of thirty degrees, having its own god and earthly ruler. Allotted their own geographical location and boundaries, the twelve houses were ruled by a god or goddess, whose jurisdiction in some instances extended to several houses. The house of the god was the entire country with the economy supporting the proper maintenance of the god's temples and rituals. The deities traversed the heavens crossing their own and each other's paths to approach or recede from the fixed stars, their movements revealing the destinies of humankind. Daily life was constructed around the utterances of the priest-kings and the various gods in whom they believed. However, the religion of the zodiac and the history of these people were so entwined it became impossible to sift one from the other, so what once had been a comprehensive map of the earth in relation to the heavens eventually resulted in a confused jumble.

The Fertile Crescent belonged to Anu. He was perceived as heaven itself. The great triad of Anu, Enlil, and Enki were worshipped as the premier deities, their influence shaping the charting of the zodiac. Many of the gods and goddesses were anthropomorphic, recalling Ishtar in particular, in her role as Sargon's lover and protector.

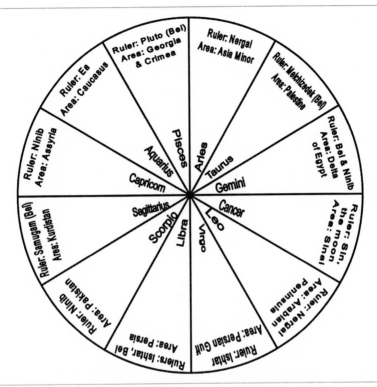

The first house is Aries, Nisan of the sacred calendar, incorporating Asia Minor. Khumbaba the sheep goddess is its mother goddess. Known also as the beautiful Aphrodite, as goddess of death in life, she renews her virginity in the sea. Her young son Eros or Ares later becomes Nergal the ruler, ruling here as the Young One. Nergal was also the god of plagues, wars, and death, so sometimes he appears as a glowing handsome youth but at others, has a very warlike demeanor.

Shamash reappears in Aries, signifying the return of spring and renewal of life, and begins the journey through the zodiacal cycle once more.

Taurus, the second house, the second month of the sacred year, is Palestine extending from the Taurus Mountains to Moab (where Mt. Nebo will be the landmark for Gemini) and included the islands of Cyprus, Crete, and Rhodes. Bel, its ruler, is Melchizedek here. His wife is Ishtar/Belit, and this was undoubtedly the house of the worship of Ishtar, who in alliance with Bel, together rule this house. The Amorites called themselves the Sons of Bel and Ishtar. Tau in Kabbalah is Jupiter or Zeus, and as Zeus (the Greek name for Bel), he took the form of the bull, the sign for this house. The feast of Taurus was celebrated as Maya, and the Beltane festival was held when the moon reached fifteen degrees in Taurus. This was the land of commerce.

Gemini is the house of the twins, Sivan being the sacred name for the month of June. The area of Gemini is the delta of Egypt and included Mt. Nebo. This land was Neter Ta- the Netherworld, the divine land, where the inhabitants were called Hiru Shaitu (in Hebrew, Shittim) the sons of Hera. Hebe was the mother goddess and Heracles received her as his bride among the immortals. Nebo rules this house, where the people were builders and artisans. The first great twins of Gemini are Jupiter/Bel and Saturn/Ninib. Both these gods ranked as fifty degrees and thus were equal rulers. Castor and Pollux, Cain and Abel, and Inanna and Utu are just some of the other famous twins. The Heraclids (the Amurru and the Hurri) are the heavenly twins. This house represents the duality in life: the good and evil aspects of humankind, and the positive and negative forces of nature.

Cancer-Ganzir, the mansion of the moon is Sinai. In the sacred calendar, Cancer is H or Heth, the fourth house, ruled by the moon/sin. The Serpent Mountains of Sinai mark the netherworld below the meridian, the lands stretching from Mt. Sinai to the Mountains of the Moon in Egypt. The oldest race in history survived here. The princes of the Serpent Mountain lived and traded in this region long before the rule of the first dynasties of Egypt. The alphabet was formed at Sinai, where a large temple stood for the goddess Beltis, known as Hathor in this region. Here Nergal enters his house as the lord of death, for this is the house of plague and pestilence. In Egyptian mythology, by initiation with water, Cancer represented the gate of souls into incarnation. A region of wonderful achievements by humankind, its people established a formidable power, controlling as they did, the commerce of land and sea. This house represents all crustaceans.

Leo covers the Arabian Peninsula as far as the Persian Gulf including all of Abyssinia, where the Straits of Hormuz (Hermes) marks the next house. The house of Leo, the sun is at its zenith, is where the sun is the lord of all. Nergal dominates the scene yet again. Here the killing heat of the summer sun and the famine from lack of rain for the scorched earth makes him the sun of death and plague.

Virgo, whose realm is the Persian Gulf, represents Woman in the zodiac. Ishtar, the ruler here, was Circe, goddess of the circle, and Ereshkigal, the great earth mother. She is the young virgin Anat, Queen of Heaven, wife of Anu. Eventually Ishtar as the great bride and mother, brought down from heaven, rules with Nebo who is exalted in this house. On her negative side, she rules Taurus. In Virgo, Ishtar's symbol is a sheaf of corn, for this was the time for marriage and the sowing of the seed.

Ishtar also ruled the house of Libra that extended through Elam/Persia. The negative side of Venus rules with Bel in Taurus, but he joins with Ishtar in Libra, creating the balance. The constellation of Libra was Aquila the eagle, with Ninib as the winged eagle of the four cherubim. The goddess of justice, Artemis, has the scales for her symbol. This was also the symbol for the Medes and Persians whose area it was. Who has not heard of the laws of the Medes and Persians—the deeds of a person weighed in the balance? This area was the house of the double eagle. Snake worship, magic, black pottery, and the potter's wheel are all associated with Libra. The pictorial sign for Libra represents the setting sun.

The eighth house is Scorpio covering Pakistan, and it is here that Saturn is at his peak or exaltation. Saturn represented by Ninib the patron god of Assyria, rules Scorpio. In the *Epic of Gilgamesh*, the Men of Mashu are the infamous scorpion gods, who guard the gates to the underworld. Sirius sets in Scorpio.

Sagittarius, the ninth house, is the house of the warrior, whose gods are Castor and Pollux. The constellation of Sagittarius roughly compares to the earthly boundaries of Sagartum now Kurdistan. Bel, as Samugan, god of cattle, is the ruler. This is the house of the Sagittari. The first representation would be Enkidu, half man and half bull. Here are the fierce warrior horsemen, the Kazalla/Kassites, who introduced horses into Mesopotamia and Egypt. When the Parthians were in power, the Sagittari, the lesser nobility, furnished the light cavalry for which the Parthian army became famous. The Kazalla were the first mercenary soldiers and their battleaxes, Sagitta, were sacred to them. The Sagittari and the Centauri were racial brothers and renowned mounted bowmen. Horses, so vitally important to these people and held in such high esteem, were sent into the afterlife with their owners. The method of royal burial was gruesome. The king with his whole court was buried under a mound. A year later, warriors on horseback encircled the mound, and then suffered a grisly fate. Stakes were driven through both warrior and horse, and in this manner, the carousel had its origins. This was the land of Lullabi and these people controlled the trade routes to the east, supplying lapis lazuli. Naram–Sin went there to continue charting the zodiac, in his effort to control trade. His reverence for Ishtar is portrayed in bas reliefs of her and her symbols found on certain cliffs in this area. The unicorn—part horse, part goat—is a composite of Sagittarius and Capricorn, the horse with one horn.

Capricorn, the tenth house, is Assyria whose ruler is Ninib/Chronus/ Saturn. Capricorn is the house to which all go to await judgment before moving into the house of Aquarius, commencing their journey around the zodiac once more. One of the symbols for this house is the scythe which is used by the grey-haired Ninib to disperse the house of Anu. Ninib was the oldest of the gods and acted as judge. The wigs worn in some courtrooms today might have their origins in this legend. Capricorn is Ifre, Khabiri, Kapra, Kopru, and Keupri.

Aquarius, the House of the Cup, of Creation and of Anu, is the eleventh house, covering the Caucasus. Although Aquarius belongs to Anu it is Ea, the god of water, who actually rules this realm. Later, Ea's son Nebo becomes lord of Aquarius. Nebo is the symbol of creation. This is the house of Adanu, which in Babylonian translates as First Man. In *The Texts of Ugarit* Asherah, the earth mother and mother goddess of this house visits her son El, who sits on the throne of the seas between the two great deeps, the Black and Caspian Seas. Asherah held the cup for the gods because Aquarius is the house of eternal life, the house of heaven. Before attaining kingship, as the cupbearer to king Ur-Zababa, Sargon was reputed to be the first mortal cup bearer. The legends of Sargon link him to this house, with his seal depicting Aquarius watering the bull/earth. There are seven seals to the fountain of life, so one must travel through seven constellations to reach Aquarius. The Aurora Borealis or Northern Lights, seen from northern Mesopotamia, appear from behind the Caucasus. Called the Girdle of Venus, they honor Ishtar.

The house of Pisces, Adar, is the twelfth month of the sacred year. This house has many names: the house of death and resurrection, the house of loaves and fishes, house of stones, and the house of many rivers. Jesus represents Pisces. Anu, holding the rank of sixty degrees as he does, joins the two houses of Aquarius and Pisces, resulting as it were, in two circles overlapping, creating the sign of the fish. The realm of Pisces is Georgia and the Crimea. Georgia is the Gorgon and the goddess is Medea. The serpents in her head are the many rivers that arise in this part of the world. The Medes, the tribe of Saguna, kept their hair long and wore scarlet kilts. Their father god was Diomedes.

Pisces is called the land of Limbo and the land of the Golden Fleece, whose ruler is Bel, known now as Pluto or Hades. This is Quoph or Qaf in Arabic and Pisces in Kabbalah. Qaf in Arabic means encircling range, beyond which is the cosmic ocean, and according to the Koran, is the mountain range encircling the world. It is the home of jinn, giants, and fairies, and was the summit of the known world.

Mysteries and rituals have had such an extraordinary hold on so many cultures, from the dawn of history throughout the ages. Prominent figures have used the science of astrology to further their wisdom, conquer lands, manipulate others, and influence lives from the lowest to the highest degree. Melchizedek, Abraham, Pythagoras, philosophers, and theologians illuminate the stage of the world, leaving their indelible imprint. The ancient mystical theories, which were gradually supplemented and incorporated into contemporary religious rites, developed from the zodiacal religion of yesteryear. The traces remain, linking us inexorably to our ancestors. The zodiac served as a form of worship, a beacon glowing in the darkness. It survives as perhaps one of the finest gifts ever bestowed upon humankind.

Glossary

Adam: First Man. House of Aries. Remnant of Cro-Magnon, Aurignacians, Amurru Hebrew "Red Earth."

Adapa: Babylonian primeval man. He introduced the worship of the gods.

Adar: Twelfth month of the sacred year. The House of Pisces.

Adonai: "Most High Lord of Hosts." Adam. God of Spring.

Adonai-Zedec: "Lord of the Zodiac." An Amorite king of Jerusalem.

Ahura Mazda: God representing goodness and light in the Zoroastrian and Mithraism religions.

Allat: Wife of Nergal—Sumerian Ereshkigal.

Allah-Nebi: Arabic name for Moses.

Amurru: Amorites. First and foremost of the great tribes of Mesopotamia.

An: Heliopolis in Egypt. One of the oldest centers for worship, reputed for its healing waters. Built by Ptah, one of two judicial Great Courts, Thebes is the other.

An: Sumerian for Anu, the "Father of the Gods."

Ana Anu: Heaven itself. "Spirit of Heaven, Ziana." Supreme Ruler.

Anahita: Persian "Lady of Celestial Waters."

Anak: Anakim, the three Sons of Anak—the Amurru, Hurri, and Shasu. Hua, Shua, Koa.

Anat: Lady of Heaven. Wife of Anu duplicated by him.

Angra Mainyu: Persian god representing darkness and evil. Twin of Ahura Mazda.

Annunaki: Assembly of the Gods. Judges of the Underworld.

Aphrodite: Ishtar in Pisces. Goddess of Death in Life, she renews her virginity in the sea. Egyptian Hamhit.

Apollo: Ninib in Capricorn. Saturn/Aplu.

Aquarius: The eleventh House of the zodiac. The Water Bearer. House of the Cup. The region of the Caucasus. The Grand Man of the Zodiac.

Aquila: Great fixed star. Scorpio. Eagle.

Ararat: Summit of the Earth. In Akkadian the twin peaks of Ararat is Mashu—the Twins.

Aries: The first House of the zodiac. Asia Minor. Nisan of the sacred calendar.

Artemis: The moon daughter of the sun. Goddess of Justice represented by the scales of Libra: The Huntress.

Asar-Luhi: Son of Enki/Ea. The "All-Seeing." Babylonian Marduk. Egyptian Osiris.

Asherah: Earth Mother. Greek Hera. Exalted in Pisces.

Ashbanipal: King of Assyria 668 BC. Learned scholar maintained that the gift of writing was bestowed upon him by the gods.

Asshur: National god of the Assyrians.

Astarte: Goddess of the Moon. Ashtoreth, Ishtar, Venus. Supreme goddess of the Phoenicians.

Astrae: Queen of Heaven of all stars. Venus. Ishtar. Saxon Eastre. Easter.

Atalanta: In Sumerian mythology the fastest moving planet—the moon, who on her journey around the zodiac, changes her shape each month.

Athur: God of Artificial Irrigation. Terrestrial deity.

Atlantis: The great Saturnian continent, the area north of the zodiac. Saturn/Chronus is the ruler.

Azariah: Chief Priest of the House of Zadok, and the ruler of the House of God.

Ba'al: Canaanite god—"Lord on High."

Ba'al-Bek: Place of Bel. Built by Nimrod or Cain.

Babbar: Shamash. The sun.

Ba'Bel: God-gate.

Babylon: Bab-gate, Ilu- of the gods. Kassite Bab Alam.

Bau: Goddess of Aquarius. "The lady who brings the dead back to life."

Beehive tombs: Made by the Lords of the Sands, the Amurru. Constructed without mortar. Found in Egypt, Balearic Islands, and

Scotland.

Bel: Lord of the Zodiac. Melchizedek. Zeus, Jupiter, Earth, Zedek, Sutekh, Marduk. Son of Ea. Supreme god of the Babylonians.

Belial: Prince of Darkness. His opposite is Michael or Melchizedek.

Belit: Wife of Bel, but at night known a Ishtar. A goddess of the Amurru. Ninlilla.

Berosus: Historian warned by Chronus of an impending flood.

Beth: House.

Bethel: Site of a great college for the priesthood. Beth-El—House of God.

Biru: Districts or boroughs defined in a zodiacal map by Sargon 1st.

Bit-Adini: Eden. North Syria. The House of Adanu.

Black Sea: Area of the House of Pisces.

Boaz: One of the two Pillars of Solomon's Temple. Represented feminine, negative, righteous, and priestly. Also known as Mishpat.

Byblos: Ancient capital of the Amurru in Phoenicia. Religious center and port.

Cancer: Fourth House of the zodiac. The region is Sinai. Sign: scarab or crab.

Capricorn: The tenth House. Assyria. The House of the Goat.

Celestial Queen of Heaven: The Moon/ Nannar.

Gate of the Gods: Bab-Ilu—Babylon. Babba/house. Ilu/god. Ilani/ the gods. El/God.

Centaurs: Found in the area of the House of Sagittarius.

Charon: Shiron—Ferryman across the Styx. Guide of souls, who represented music, medicine, shooting, plants and medicinal herbs.

Children of Eden: One of the titles for the Amurru and Hurri.

Children of the Gods: The Gauls called themselves Children of Dis (Anu).

Children of the Third Son: Cain, Abel, and Seth. The Amurru, Hurri, and Kassites.

Chronus: Saturn/Ninib. Enki/Ea. Ruler of Capricorn.

Cimmerians: Sumerians, Crimeans, Tuari, Tartars. They dwelt near Hades, the Black Sea. Greeks called them "Creatures of Hel."
Circe: Goddess of the Circle. Daughter of the Sun The myths of Circe turning men into animals stem from the zodiac and the many animals placed in it.
Curetes: Armed companions of the sacred king. Young men with shaved heads. Priest-assistants of the worshippers of Bel.
Cyrus: Of the House of Teispis, indicating he was of the Hurrian royal house. A Son of Dis, his tomb was a copy of a Hurrian temple, a forerunner of modern churches.

Decans: Ruler of ten degrees of a zodiacal sign, each zodiacal house is divided into thirty degrees. Signs.
Demons: Dymani, Daha—nomadic Medes, priests, Magi. As the constellations appeared, thought to be demons arising from the underworld, Satani Dar, "The Place of Satan."
Dionysus: God of the Vine. Dio Nisa/ Iacchus/Bacchus. The Goat/ Capricorn is associated with him.
Dis: Early word for God. Anu.
Druids: Priests of the Celtic nations. Dryads.
Dumuzi: A Shepherd King who married Ishtar/Inanna. Tammuz.
Dur: Place or fort.

Ea: Babylonian God of Supreme Wisdom, Spells and Charms. His earthly city was Eridu. Sumerian Enki.
Eden: E.Din. "The Abode of the Righteous Ones." The first House of Adam.
Edom: According to the Hebrews, the kings of Edom were symbolic of a world formless and void, thus ruling before the formation of the zodiac.
El: El Elyon—a Canaanite god.
Enki: Sumerian god of wisdom. Ea.
Enkidu: En is An or heaven. Ki is earth. Du is to go, walk or move.

Enkidu is a composite of Man/Adam/Earth. In another aspect he is the friend of Gilgamesh. Possibly the centaur of Sagittarius.

Enlil: A son of Anu. Lord of the Wind. "King of all the Lands."

Enmerkar: A priest-king of Uruk, who, according to Sumerian epic poetry, was the first king to record his words on a clay tablet.

Enoch: One of ten antediluvian patriarchs reputed to have "walked with God." Regarded as one of the legendary founders of the Freemasons.

Enuma Elish: Babylonian epic poem of creation.

Ereshkigal: Great Earth Mother. Persephone. Wife to Nergal, granddaughter of Enlil. El Arish, queen of the Netherworld, Taurus and Scorpio, below the dividing line in the zodiac.

Eridu: First earthly dwelling of the gods, and the first city of the Sumerian kingships. This city belonged to Enki, and was built near the head of the Persian Gulf.

Eros: The young Ares. Son of Bel and Venus. Born and exalted in Pisces.

Eve: Consort of Adad, the storm god. Iveh, Asherah, Hera. The Lady Hurri/Khiva/Hiva. Also associated with Ninkharsag, the Great Mother Goddess.

Ezekiel: Prophet and priest of the Temple of Yahweh, who established the rules of priesthood, with Zadok as the chief priest. Ezekiel's vision was of Yahweh's return entering his House through the "Gate of Righteousness," Tsedeq.

Four Cherubim of Kaballah: Earth, Sun, Air and Water: represented by the four astral gods: Earth—Jupiter/Bel/Taurus; Sun—Mars/Nergal/Leo; Air—Saturn/Ninib/Scorpio; Water- Mercury/Nebo/Aquarius.

Geb: "Who Piles Up The Earth." "The Stretched Out Firmament." Geb and Nut were one of the Divine Couples of the Guardians of Egypt, and reigned over it. The Father and Mother of the Gods. Their four children: Osiris, Isis, Seth and Nephtys.

Gemini: The third House. The Delta of Egypt.

Gilgamesh: The Great Sun of the Circle. Hero of the Zodiac. He was addressed as "Offspring of the Gods." The oldest tablets of this epic were found at Nippur.

Hadd: Hades, where Bel, when in Pisces, is imprisoned for the odd days of the zodiacal year.

Hamhit: "The Powerful One of Mendes." Wife of the god of the temple of Ram. Lady of Heaven, queen of all the gods. Represented by a pillar with a fish, on top of her head. Venus in Pisces.

Hathor: Egyptian Mother Goddess. Lady of the Pillar (Tefnut). Lady of the Sky, Lady of Turquoise.

Heaven: Heofan. Hof = House of Anu. The Caucasus in the zodiacal map of the Earth.

Hebe: Great Earth Mother. Daughter of Zeus and Hera. Heracles received Hebe as his bride among the immortals, from Hebt, Egypt. Called Juventas by the Romans, who believed she had the power to restore youth.

Hecate: Greek Earth goddess of fertility and magical power. Associated with the lower world of ghosts, demons, magic, and sorcery. Goddess of the New Year.

Hehu: God of Eternity.

Hel: Goddess of Death.

Hera: Wife of Zeus.

Heracles: Hero of the Zodiac, and of the Heraclidae. In Greek mythology he was Hercules with twelve labors to perform.

Heraclids: Amurru and Hurri. (Amorites/Horites)

Hermes: Ruler of the Underworld in the zodiac. Babylonian Nebo. Ruler of Gemini and Virgo. Inventor of astronomy, architecture, medicine, and writing. Identified with Nebo and Thoth and Mercury.

Heth: July in the Sacred Calendar. In the zodiac it is Cancer. The name Hittite stems from this and the Hittites were known as the Sons of Heth.

Horus: Son of Osiris and Isis. First ruler of all Egypt.

Horus of the Horizon: The Sun God of the Egyptians.

Hyksos: Desert Kings. Shepherd Kings. The Avars.

Inanna: Sumerian for Ishtar/Venus.

Irra: Nergal/Ares/Mars.

Ishtar: Babylonian goddess of love and war. Known as Venus at night, Belit by day.

Issacer: Prophets who accompanied the armies to interpret the signs of heaven. Nostradamus of Issacer.

Isis: Egyptian Queen of Heaven.

Jachin: One of the twin pillars (the other Boaz), which stood outside the Temple of Solomon. Represented all things masculine, positive, establishment, stability and kingly. When united with the other pillar, Boaz, by the holy arch, Shalom becomes the "Gate of Righteousness." The two pillars represented the kingly and priestly aspects of the state. Jachin also referred to as Tsedeq—Teacher of Righteousness.

James The Just: Tsedeq, the priestly messiah. Brother of Jesus of Nazareth.

Janus: "The God Who Looks Both Ways." The two-faced god. The most ancient and revered god of the Romans, putting him even before Jupiter. Shown on cylinder seal of Sumer as Isimud, servant of Enki. Janus Quirinius—guardian deity of the gates.

Khumbaba: Mother Goddess of Aries. Sheep goddess.

Jupiter: Bel's planet. Jupiter in Cancer is in the House of his exaltation.

Kaballah: The hidden teachings of the Essenes of the Qumran community.

Kazalla: Kislev in the Sacred Calendar. Sagartum. The Kazalla were the first mercenary soldiers.

Kerche: "Her Place," that of Circe, Goddess of the Circle.

Khab: Stars in the map of heaven.

Khabiri: Nomadic people, who could not be relegated to one god or planet, nicknamed the Wanderers. Egyptians called the Hebrews by this name.

Khabirim: Divine group of seven Khabirim (Mighty Ones), created by the Phoenicians. Sydyk was Lord of All Seven. An eighth Khabir, Eshmun, was added, who ranked higher than the rest.

Khadeshim: Representatives of the god of the sanctuary at the summit of the ziggurat in Babylon. Possibly the children of the ritual marriage of the Great Bride, Virgo. The sons would be in the most holy hereditary priesthood.

Kirk/Ninkarrak, goddess of Sumer and Elam.

Knights Templar: Order founded by Hugues de Paynes to protect Christian pilgrims in the Holy Land.

Koretes: Demigods, armed with bronze weapons, they were commissioned by Rhea to protect Zeus. They taught the Cretans agriculture and metalworking. The Koretes performed wild war dances that earned them the title of "Noisy Worshippers of Bel."

Lady of the Serpent Mountain: Ninkharsag.

Laphria: A goat king. The goat cult preceded the cult of the bull in Crete. Earliest signs of the cult were found in the burial ground of a Neanderthal boy.

Laz: Another name for the wife of Nergal, Lord of the Dead.

Leo: The fifth House, and the throne or strong House of the Sun. In the Sacred Calendar—Ab or Ib. Egypt and Ethiopia to the Persian Gulf.

Libra: The seventh House. Elam/Persia.

Loki: Ancient Syrian god, meaning "First Man." Luck, Leakey, Lucca, Luke. The House of the Lamb, God of the Vikings.

Lord of the Zodiac: Jupiter/Zeus/Bel. Other names: Zedec, Sadok, Sydyk, Sutekh. The names for Amorite priest-kings were Adonai-Zedec (Lord of Justice) and Melchi-Zedec.

Lords of the Sands: The Amurru, Princes of Siut. God of Siut is Uapaitre/Jupiter/Bel.

Luke: Priests were called Lucumones, priest-kings. The first gods of the Babylonian epic were Lukmu and Lakamu. Loki or Lake was the Amurru in north Syria.

Ma'at: Goddess of Truth, Justice and Order, moral and physical. Daughter of Ra, identical with Themis/Libra.

Magi: Hereditary priesthood. Priests of Bel. Median priests and astrologers.

Mah: Great Star of Capricorn.

Marduk: God of Thunderstorms. Bel. He was acknowledged as creator of the universe and of humankind, the god of light and life, and the ruler of destinies. He assigned the sky to Anu, the air and surface of the earth to Enlil, and the waters in and on the land to Ea. Canaanite Ba'al, Sumerian Asar.

Mashu: One of the peaks of Ararat. Boundary line of the Underworld.

Mazzaloth: Circle of the Zodiac.

Masloth: Twelve signs.

Medes: Sons of Marchesvan—Scorpio.

Me's: Divine laws of the gods governing the universe.

Melchizedek: Amorite name for their priest-kings. Priest-king of Jerusalem. One of Bel's many names as Lord of the Zodiac.

Melki Ashapu: Lord of Seers or Prophets.

Men of Mashu: Giants/gods who guarded the gates to the Underworld.

Mercury: Messenger of the gods. A "rain maker," and go-between. Nebo.

Merodach: Merudug/Marduk. He instituted the year, dividing it into twelve months, each month with three decans each of which exercised its influence for a period of ten days. This was placed under the authority of Nibiru, the "Ferryman."

Mishpat: (See Boaz.)

Mistletoe: Sacred to the Druids, as an all-healer, and because it grows mainly on oak trees, dedicated to Bel. The round fruit resembles the planets.

Mithras: Persian god of contracts, friendship and fertility.

Moon: Nannar. The Measure of Time changing her shape each part of the month. The Queen of Heaven who "owns" the stars and the planets.

Moon's Path: The path of the moon across the sky. A zodiacal belt twelve degrees wide within which move the sun, moon, and all the planets.

Moses: Arabic name for Moses is "Allah Nebi," the god Nebo.

Mot: Death in Arabic; Latin: Mort. House of Death is Pisces. Mitra— Sun of Death.

Nannar: Sin. The moon. When the earth and sky had been divided, all things had been allotted their places, with the exception of the ship and a "House" for seafarers. Nannar became the ship god of the sky, exalted in Taurus and ruler of Cancer.

Nannar-Sin: Firstborn earthly son of Enlil, remembered for his achievement establishing the great city of Ur as a thriving metropolis.

Nebo: The Winged Man of the Zodiac. God of water, intellect, and medicine. Nebo in Aquarius is the symbol of creation. Associated with Thoth and Hermes.

Nemesis: Fate. Her wheel of fortune is the chart of the zodiac as the constellations rise.

Nergal: God of plague, war and death.

Nephilim: "Those who descended."

Neter Ta: The Underworld. Ereshkigal is queen of this realm. Leo is Lord of the Underworld at the bottom of the zodiac, and Anu, Lord of Heaven at the top.

Niburu: The Ferryman. One of the seven outer planets, known to the Sumerians as the Planet of the Crossing, and the home of Anu. Its symbol is the cross. In the Enuma Elish, Niburu crosses the path of Ti'amat.

Ninib: Lord of Justice and Air.

Ninkharsag: Mother Goddess.

Ninurta: Son of Enlil and Sud (Ninkharsag), Akkadian Urash, Possessor of Divine Powers. The god who taught farming. His spouse was Bau, goddess of poultry.

Nippur: Sumer's religious center where the calendar of the relationship between the sun, moon and the earth was created around 3880 BC. Clay tablets found at Nippur revealed many astronomical terms.

Nisrock: The eagle of Libra and Scorpio, which, at first, were combined into one House. The balance was the claws of the eagle. Symbol of Ninib.

Osiris: Egyptian "God the Father." Ruler of the kingdom of the dead. Son of the goddess Nut, he ruled Egypt with his sister/consort Isis.

Pan: Eros, son of Zeus/Bel, and Virgo in Pisces.

Pillars: Created to "reach to the heavens." Jacob in Sumerian means pillar.

Pillars of the Freemasons: Jachin/Tsedeq; Boaz/Mishpat.

Princes of the Serpent Mountain: Amurru, Hurri, Kassites.

Ptah: Egyptian Enki. "The Developer." Engineer, architect, and scientist. He built the sacred city of An (Heliopolis).

Proteus: A sea deity, said to be the first man. Son of Oceanus (Ea) and Tethys. Neptune gave him the gift of prophecy. Oceanus incorporates Anu and Ea.

Ra: Son of Ptah. "The Holy One." The "Falcon of the Horizon." His celestial boat traversed the heavens.

Reseph: Rest, Saturn. As the seventh planet Rest, he is called Great God and Lord of Heaven.

Rhea: Goddess of Capricorn.

Rosslyn Chapel: Mystical building in Scotland.

Sabat: Sabbath. Holy day. Seventh day.

Sagittarius: The ninth month whose House is the area of Kurdistan.

Samech/Samugan: God of Cattle.

Sargon 1st: The world's first emperor. Creator of the earthly map of the zodiac.

Saturn: Satan. Cast out of heaven when Nebo became Lord of Aquarius in 747 BC. Saturn is El or Chronus, who, according to the Texts of Ugarit, dwelt between "the two great deeps," the Black and Caspian Seas. The first mention of Saturn is as Sataran, god of the Lullabi. The Grim Reaper, who gathers souls in Capricorn.

Scorpio: The seventh and last planet to appear in the zodiac. Pakistan.

Scorpion Men: Heroes of the Zodiac. (See Mashu Men.)

Sea of the Sunrise: The Caspian Sea. Ninib was the god of the rising and setting sun.

Sekhet: Lioness, Leonine. As the Lioness, she is the wife of Nergal in Leo.

Serpent: Symbol in the zodiac for eternal life.

Seth: The third son of Adam. Son of the god Geb, and the goddess, Nut. Worshipped as a god by the Hyksos at Tanis. This god was also Sutekh, Zedec and Sataran. Revered by some, but later came to be thought of as evil.

Shamash: The Sun/Helios. The symbol for Shamash is the lion, because his House is Leo. His divine symbol was the equal-armed cross, which later became Nebo's symbol. Saturn shared the name of Shamash as the star of the sun. He ruled over the city of Shulim, Ur-Shulim (Jerusalem).

Shalom: Holy Arch—Gate of Righteousness.

Shua: Persians.

Sinai: Cancer in the Sacred Calendar. In the alphabet is Heth. The first alphabet was found at Sinai.

Sirius: The Dog Star, Canis Major, the Dog of Orion. The Amurru were called Sons of Senir/Sirius. Suriash, god of the Kassites.

Sivan: Gemini/June in the Sacred Calendar.

Sons of Anak: The Three Sons of Anak were the Hua/Hurrians; Shua/Khassa; Koa/Kumanni. In addition, the Phoenicians, as part of the Chaldean family were Sons of Anak. The lived and ruled in Mesopotamia, Egypt and the islands of the Persian Gulf. Astrology, metalworking, astronomy and trading were common to all.

Sons of Anu: In Assyrians inscriptions, the Martu.

Sons of Hera: Pre-dynastic Egyptians known as the Dioscuri.

Sphinx: Egyptian edifice marking the four cardinal points.
Stelae: Stele. Pictorial calendars of the zodiacal or sacred year.
Tablets of Destiny.
Stone of Hercules: Stone of the Heraclids. A "kalamitah" magnetic
stone, cardinal point.
Sud: Daughter of Anu. As the wife of Enlil, called Ninlil, Ninmah.
Mother of Gods.
Tammuz: God of July, lover of Ishtar.
Tartarus: Hades.
Tartary: Another name for Hell.
Tau: Last letter of the Hebrew alphabet. Mark. Tau cross represents
king, priest and prophet. The Triple Tau: Temple of Jerusalem; Holy
of Holies; Temple of Yahweh.
Taurus: The second House and month of the sacred year. Palestine.
The Bull.
Thoth: Premier Egyptian god. Brother of Marduk and Ma'at. Lord
of the Sacred Words. God of astronomy, magic, mathematics, and
botany. God of sciences who taught the Egyptians the art of building.
Tehuti: He Who Balances.
Ti'amat: Babylonian name for waste of waters and chaos from
which the gods descended. The universal primeval mother goddess
Ti'amat who was slain by Marduk.
Tiglath-Pileser: Assyrian king known for his devotion to the gods of
the zodiac.
Tower of Babel: Seven-storey ziggurat built to honor Marduk/Bel.
Triad of Babylonia: The premier gods: Anu, Bel and Ea.
Triad of Goddesses: The foremost goddesses: Anat, Asherah and Ishtar.
Tzaddi: Q in the Hebrew alphabet. Zedec.
Tsedeq: One of two Pillars of Solomon's Temple and of Freemasonry.
UL.HE: Sumerian for Shiny Herd.
Unicorn: Part horse- part goat. Sagittarius and Capricorn, a composite
for when the sun is on the cusp of both Houses.
Uranus: Anu or Ur. Father of Poseidon. Ur is north.
Ursa: Mother Goddess of Helvetia.
Utu: The Sun. Shamash of the Semites.

Venus: The Queen of Heaven: Ishtar. Divine symbol was the eight-pointed star. Venus and the Sun were the Heavenly Twins. Venus revered as the ruler over women. Associated with crops, the harvest and all things martial.
Virgo: The Virgin. The House of Virgo represents Woman on the zodiac. The Persian Gulf.

Winged Lion: Shamash/Leo
Winged Man: Nebo.

Yahweh: Son of El. "I Am that I Am." God of Righteousness.
Yamm:Sea god of Pisces.

Zaddik: Righteousness. Zaddik priests were teachers of Kabbalah.
Zadok: High Priest of Jerusalem. He anointed Solomon as king. Hebrew meaning "The Just." Tsedeq-Zodiac. Sons of Zadok- the Zadokites of Qumran.
Zedec: God of the Night Sky. Jupiter. Sutekh, Sadok, Sydyk—the Eighth God.
Zeus: Jupiter/Bel. Zeus first appears as Zius Udra, Spirit of the Sun, in Pisces. Zeus exalted in Cancer. Dis, Dios, Theos.
Zi: Spirit
Zi-Ana: Spirit of Heaven
Zi-Ka: Spirit of the Earth
Ziggurat: Man-made Mountain constructed as an earthly dwelling for the gods. Zi— "spirit" Spirit of Ararat.
Zodiakos Kyklos: Greek "Animal Circle." Kyklos—circle. Zoion—"animals."

Bibliography

Aivanhov,Omraam Mikael: The Zodiac, Key to Man & the Universe
Allegro, John: The Dead Sea Scrolls
Anderson, Karl: The Astrology of the Old Testament
Bames General History: Brief History of Ancient, Medieval & Modern

Boarman, John: The Greeks Overseas
Breasted: History of the Early World – Ancient Times
Broderick, M. & Morton: Concise Dictionary of Egyptian Archaeology
Bronsted, Johannes: The Vikings
Budge, E.A. Wallis: Egyptian of the Dead
Bullfinch, Thomas: Age of Fable

Caesar: Conquest of Gaul
Cambridge Ancient History: Crown of Egypt
Cambridge Ancient History: Dynasty of Agade
Cambridge Ancient History: Hammurabi, End of a Dynasty
Cambridge Ancient History: Phrygia and People of Anatolia
Cambridge Ancient History: Pre-History
Carpenter, Edward: Pagan & Christian Creeds – Their Origin
Carrington, Richard: Guide to Earth History
Ceram, C.W: Gods, Graves & Scholars

Churchill, W.: Birth of Britain
Coghlan, Ronan: The Illustrated Encyclopaedia of Arthurian Legends
Cottrell, Leonard: Anvil of Civilization
Culican, William: The First Merchant Venturers

Elwell, Walter A. (Edited by): Baker's Bible Handbook

Frankfort, Henri: Birth of Civilization in the Near East
Frazer, Sir James: The New Golden Bough
Freke, Timothy & Gandy, Peter: The Jesus Mysteries
Frye, Richard N.: The Heritage of Persia

Gardner, Laurence: Bloodline of the Holy Grail
Gaster, Theodore H.: Thespis
Gayley, Charles Mills: Classic Myths in English Literature – Based on Bulfinch
Girschmao, R.: Iran
Goodspeed, George Stephen: The History of the Babylonians & Assyrians
Gordon, Cyrus H.: Ugarit & Minoan Crete
Grant, Madison: The Passing of the Great Race
Graves, Robert: The Greek Myths, Vols. I & II
Grun, Bernard: Timetables of History
Gumey, O. R.: The Hittites
Gumont, Franz: Astrology & Religion Among the Greeks & Romans
Gumont, Franz: Mysteries of Mithra

Hadas, Moses: History of Rome
Hancock, Graham: Fingerprints of the Gods
Hardin, Donald: The Phoenicians
Hawkins, Gerald S.: Stonehenge Decoded
Heidel: The Babylonian Genesis
Herman, Paul: Conquest by Man
Herodotus: The Histories

Hinz, Rene: Cambridge Ancient History - Elam 1600-1200 BC
Hinz, Walter: Cambridge Ancient History - Persia 2400-1800 BC
Homer: The Iliad
Homer: The Odyssey
Hooke, S.J.: The Annals of Tacitus
Hutchinson, R. W.: Pre-Historic Crete

James, T.G.H.: Cambridge Ancient History - Egypt Hyksos
Jeffers, H. Paul: Freemasons
Josephus, Flavius: The Great Roman-Jewish War

Keller, Werner: The Bible as History
King James Version: The Holy Bible
Knight, Christopher & Lomas, Robert: The Hiram Key
Kramer, Noah Stanley: History Begins at Sumer
Kramer, Samuel Noel: Myths of the Ancient World

Lamb, Leonard: Hannibal
Lincoln, E.F.: Britain's Unwritten History
Lloyd, Seton: Art of Ancient Near East
Lloyd, Seton: Early Highland Peoples of Anatolia

MacKendrick, Paul: The Greek Stones Speak
Maspero, Professor: The Dawn of Civilization in Egypt & Chaldea
McEvedy, Colin: Penguin Atlas of Ancient History
McQueen, James C.: Babylon
Merrill, Unger: Archaeology & the Old Testament
Meyer, Marvin: The Gnostic Discoveries
Michell, John: The Earth Spirit
Montague, Ashley: Man & His First Million Years

Piotrozski, Hauz Zilmund: Afghanistan, Kurdistan & Urartu
Plato: Symposium Protogaros & Meno The Republic
Procopius: The Great Histories
Mankind Quarterly: People & Races of Ancient Palestine Vo. VI

Ragozin, Z.A.: Assyria
Rawlinson, George: Ancient Monarchies

Samhaber, Ernst: Merchants Make History
Sanders, N.K.: Epic of Gilgamesh
Seyffert, Oscar: Dictionary of Classical Antiquities
Silerbury, Robert: Lost Cities & Vanished Civilizations
Sinclair, Andrew: The Secret Scroll
Sitchen, Zecharia: The Wars of Gods & Men
Smith, Homer: Man and His Gods
Sykes, Egerton: Atlantis

Thorndike, Lynn: A Short History of Civilization
von Vacono, Otto Wilhelm: The Etruscans of the Ancient World

Wells, H.G.: Outline of History
Wendt, Herbert: It Began in Babel
Wilmshurst, W.L.: The Meaning of Masonry
Winstanley, P. M. & White, E.R.: Mansions of the Gods
Woolley, Sir Leonard: History of Mankind
Woolley, Sir Leonard: The Sumerians
Woolley, Sir Leonard: Ur of the Chaldees

Compact Edition of the Oxford English Dictionary—1971
The Koran
Worldwide Illustrated Encyclopedia
Xenophon's Anabasis